Long-Term care planning and Long-Term Care Insurance can both be confusing subjects. This book provides the essentials you need to know to make smart decisions with factual data and some of the best visual depictions that I've seen used. A failure to plan is a plan for failure. This is a great way to start.

—JESSE SLOME, Executive Director
American Association for Long-Term Care Insurance

It is my pleasure to convey my appreciation to Jeff Tomlin as an excellent Continuing Education instructor. Since early 2011, Jeff has offered "Long Term Care Planning" through the Successful Aging Institute here at Lane Community College. Excellent to begin with, the class continues to improve as Jeff makes adaptations based on his ongoing research and on the input he receives from his wide spectrum of adult students.

—BARBARA C. SUSMAN,
MSW, Director, Successful Aging Institute,
Lane Community College

Very informative. I've already been able to take critical actions based on this class, I've also been able to significantly help my 90+ year old Dad and Mom.

The papers, the speakers and the goodies at the last class were great. I like the fact that nothing was being sold—no pressure to buy anything.

Jeff gave us so much information about long term care insurance and hybrid products available now. The other speakers (he invited to speak to us) were great too.

Jeff was very informative and very objective in his presentations. He did not try to convince us to purchase any products.

The class was relaxed, informal, with well discussed issues about Long-Term care.

—LANE COMMUNITY COLLEGE STUDENTS

WILL I NEED LONG-TERM CARE?

Planning Guide and Workbook

JEFF TOMLIN, CLTC

WILL I NEED LONG-TERM CARE?

First Edition

Copyright © October 2012 by Jeff Tomlin

Printed in the United States of America

Contents

Preface

There are a handful of Long-Term *Care* books and Long-Term Care *Insurance* books which have been published. Some explain Medicare and Medicaid in depth. Others give you guidance in elder law issues, or in choosing a care provider or facility (aka "community"). Some explain Long-Term Care Insurance exhaustively, down to the last industry-specific contractual clause.

This book is aimed squarely at folks who have decided they need to plan ahead for care but want data: what is their risk, what does care cost where they live, what sources of funds do they have access to which will pay for care, etc. It offers an even-handed approach; there is no attempt to coerce you into buying a product or service.

This book is unique, first because of its primary purpose: to review every possible method of paying for Long-Term Care at some point in the future. It won't help you if you're currently caring for a family member, and it doesn't explain Medicaid, Medicare, or Long-Term Care Insurance *in depth*. It does give what I believe to be the relevant details of the governmental plans which help pay for care, and the private, insurance industry plans which help pay for care. It's also a resource for those who want to know if it makes sense to self-fund their care with cash or assets.

Following the review of all sources of payment, etc., the workbook will walk you through the number crunching related to setting a budget and creating a plan to pay for future Long-Term Care. The workbook is also unique.

I've dedicated a page of my website to resources related to this book. You'll find a PDF version of the workbook, so you can download and print a hard copy. Eventually I'd like to add a "self-funding calculator" spreadsheet, which will allow you to calculate various self-funding scenarios. I will update the page as other ideas crop up.

Check it out at: **www.tbplan.com/guidebook**.

I hope you find it useful.

Sincerely,
Jeff Tomlin, CLTC

Introduction

It was the second-best ride of my life. I was 450 miles from home, after a long "iron-butt" motorcycle ride with a couple buddies. We departed Eugene, Oregon, the morning of June 30 1996. At about dinner time we arrived at Wallowa Lake campground near Joseph, Oregon. I went to the pay phone at the campground to call home. My wife answered and said "you've got to call your stepmom right away." This is how family Long-Term Care events happen: suddenly, out of the blue, when you're not ready and the possibility is the last thing on your mind.

Planning helps take the guesswork out of the equation when the planned-for event occurs. Just as with fire drills or music rehearsals, people will know what to do when the time comes.

I called my stepmother and was informed that my father had suffered a stroke and was in a coma. The doctors caring for my father gave us some options. They were not confident dad would ever wake up on his own. They were willing to take the blood clot out of the carotid artery in his neck, but they told us it was likely that surgery would simply loosen up further clots and send them to his brain, compounding the issue. Other options were to leave him on life support and see if he would awake on his own, or to take him off life support. They needed a decision within the hour. My father was 66 years old, and I was 30.

We chose to continue the life support. Frankly, this was the passive, "hope things will work out" option. I regret it. Within a few weeks, my dad came out of his coma, was released from the hospital, and started to recover. Various therapists came to his home to help him in his recovery. He was already blind before his stroke. Now he was unable to speak or write, and paralyzed on his right side.

Then came another stroke. His health deteriorated for the next eight years, and he passed away in 2004 of an enlarged heart.

For those eight years, my dad was trapped inside his body with an able mind but no way to communicate.

This was hell on earth for him-and all concerned. Our family eventually came to regret the decision to leave him on life support the day he had the first stroke. Hindsight is 20-20, right?

I am an insurance agent, licensed to sell life and health insurance since 1988. In 1994 my father had asked if I could sell him some Long-Term Care Insurance. I said "sure"—and then did some research to find out what Long-Term Care Insurance was! My father had already survived a heart attack, diverticulitis, and other medical problems. Consequently, we were able to find only one company willing to issue him a policy. This company limited him to a two-year benefit of $100 per day because of his health.

After Dad's first stroke, we were able to provide him with in-home care for a while. But eventually we moved him to a facility—and then to another, and then one after another depending on room availability and his increasing need for higher levels of care. Eventually his Long-Term Care Insurance benefits were exhausted, and my stepmom began paying cash for his care. This was awkward because she was spending my stepsibling's inheritance.

Meanwhile, my brother agonized because he didn't live nearby and wasn't able to visit Dad often. I saw Dad every week—though usually only for an hour. These times were painful. I read letters from family to him and told him about things going on in my life, but he wasn't able to respond.

Those who have had experiences similar to mine say that if a family member is providing care, strong resentment and jealousy can easily crop up between siblings. Most often, the "good daughter" provides care. The other siblings see that she is handling the situation, and they think everything is OK. The good daughter will languish with the burden and pain of seeing her parent suffer and will cry out for help, but she won't usually get it. Her siblings know she's the good daughter and can be counted on to do what's right. They will, however, expect their full share of the inheritance. This can tear the family apart. I've seen it.

The emotional toll is high.

In this book you'll see the various options available to you when it comes to making financial decisions related to Long-Term Care planning. This book summarizes everything I've learned about Long-Term Care since 1994, both from inside the industry as an insurance salesman, and from outside the industry as an instructor teaching Long-Term Care planning at a community college. When you finish the book, you'll have tools to make a well informed decision.

According to data from the 2010 U.S. Census, the fastest growing demographic are those aged 85 years and older. How many years will you live, going forward from now: 20? 30? 40 years? The Census also says that a person who has attained the age of 65 will live to about age 83. How many hale, hearty 83 year olds do you know?

Due to advances in medicine, we are living longer. We also grow gradually more frail-at a slower rate than our parents did. We simply do not die suddenly, for the most part.

The initial wave of baby boomers has started to retire-the so-called "silver tsunami." Medicaid has traditionally provided Long-Term Care as a safety net for those who have extremely low income and assets. Medicaid funding, however, is being cut across the country as funds are being stretched to the limit. The bottom line is that **Medicaid benefits are not based on** ***needs*, they are based on *budgets.*** The only sure thing is change; benefits will not look the same in 20 years as they do now-and you can be pretty sure they won't be more generous.

The risk of needing care runs very high, and the potential cost can be overwhelming. Frankly, the information above has caused many of us to simply bury our heads in the sand. It's scary.

Unlike most, you've chosen to face this topic head-on. Should you put aside a few bucks every month, to save up money in case you eventually need care? Should you rely on Medicaid? Should you look into a reverse mortgage? VA benefits? Should you transfer the financial risk to a 3rd party via Long-Term Care Insurance? By the time you finish reading my book and have completed the exercises in the workbook section, you'll be well informed and should be able to set a course for the future. If you're reading this, it implies you're not afraid to face the fact that most likely you will need care. What has brought you to this point?

Perhaps your family has already been impacted by a Long-Term Care event, and you're not sure what to do. Maybe you're planning ahead so you can enjoy some peace of mind, knowing that you have already made important decisions and plans. Perhaps you have never seriously considered Long-Term Care, and you'd just like to get a little more information.

Regardless of your situation, the time to think about Long-Term Care is now. Most healthy people don't need Long-Term Care until they are in their eighties, however, illness and injury can strike anytime. Long-term care costs will continue to escalate, so the smart choice is to determine a plan of action as soon as possible.

I created this book to walk you through every possible method of paying for Long-Term Care—through VA benefits, Medicare, Medicaid, reverse mortgages, Long-Term Care Insurance, the new hybrid (aka linked-benefit) insurance, Life Settlements and Viatical Settlements.

If you need Long-Term Care someday from a professional, will you be willing and able to pay cash for it? Could you write a check for $5,000 to $8,000 every month?

Will you instead ask your spouse to care for you, even though you see the toll it takes on him or her, because you are worried about the possibility of spending *all* the money you worked so hard to save? Does your family believe it to be appropriate and/or ethical that a paid caregiver care for you, given that you may have children, spouse or family in the area? Have you ever thought about this? Did you know that the risk of mental health problems increases by as much as 50 percent for family caregivers?[1] If your kid skins his knees, you give him a band aid. If he breaks his leg, do you try to take care of it yourself, or turn to a professional?

Perhaps your kids are willing to care for you. Are *YOU* willing to ask your children to put their busy lives on hold, quit their jobs, and/or move into the area to take care of you? Did you know that 63% of primary family caregivers report a loss of household income, average of 23%?[2] In fact, according to a study by the National Center on Women and Aging, caregivers lose an *average* of $659,130 over their lifetime in reduced salary and benefits.[3]

Here's one of the issues in a nutshell, regarding professional care: Can you become a spender-after a lifetime of being a saver? Switching gears is not as easy as it might sound. Would it be easier to spend OPM (other people's money, or insurance) for care instead of YOM (your own money). OPM is addictive!

This guide is primarily about paying for care. It's aimed at people who are already convinced they need to delve into this topic.

Bear in mind, however, that the primary reason to plan ahead for Long-Term Care financing is not financial; it's emotional. It's about family dynamics and interactions. The worst toll taken by Long-Term Care is the relational-emotional toll. A great source of further information on the family dynamics of Long-Term Care is "Beyond Dollars" from Genworth.[4]

1

Defining the Problem

O ver the last few decades we've all heard that "improvements in medical care will lead to longer, healthier lives." Unfortunately, that statement is only partially true. Yes, we are living longer lives, but not necessarily healthier. We are healthy longer, but we are also sicker longer. Modern medicine extends our lives, but we tend to suffer a gradual, painful decline in our health before we pass on. It didn't used to be this way, even 10–20 years ago. This has been called the *frailing* of America, and it means that *most* of us are likely to require Long-Term Care.

THE DEFINITION OF LONG-TERM CARE

Long-term care includes a variety of services and support systems to meet health or personal-care needs for an extended period. Most Long-Term Care is non-skilled, personal-care assistance, or help with activities of daily living (ADLs), such as these:

- Bathing

- Dressing

- Transferring (from bed or chair)

- Using the toilet

- Caring for incontinence

- Eating

- The need for care may arise due to one of these physical impairments, or a cognitive impairment such as dementia.

The goal of Long-Term Care services is to help you maximize your independence and functionality at a time when you are unable to be fully independent. Planning ahead will give you more control over whether you'll stay at home to receive care, or in a facility.

HOW MUCH CARE WILL I NEED?

Distribution and duration of Long-Term Care services (for a 65 year old).[5]

TYPE OF CARE	AVERAGE NUMBER OF YEARS PEOPLE USE THIS TYPE OF CARE	PERCENT OF PEOPLE WHO USE THIS TYPE OF CARE (%)
Any Services		
	3 years	69
At Home		
Unpaid care only	1 year	59
Paid care	Less than 1 year	42
Any care at home	2 years	65
In Facilities		
Nursing facilities	1 year	35
Assisted living	Less than 1 year	13
Any care in facilities	1 year	37

This table from Longtermcare.gov blends male and female statistics together. We'll break it down by gender in the next chapter. While about one-third of today's 65-year-olds may never need Long-Term Care services and supports, 20 percent will need care for *longer* than 5 years.

2

Are the Odds Stacked Against me?

Nearly 70 percent of 65-year-olds will require some type of Long-Term Care services during their lifetime. Over 35 percent will need care in a nursing home for some period of time. Service and support needs vary from one person to the next and often change over time. Women need care for longer (3.7 years) than do men (2.2 years). A third of today's 65-year-olds may never need Long-Term Care services, but 20 percent of them will need care for more than five years.[6]

You're not off the hook if you are younger: 40 percent of care in the U.S. is received by people under the age of 65. The diagram on the next shows the risk that a 65-year-old will require Long-Term Care. If you are younger than age 65, you are even *more* likely to eventually need care if you live from now 'til beyond 65.

Why are women more likely to need care and for a longer period? Women live longer than men, and women tend to be more able than men to handle the confinement and lack of independence that comes with needing care.

The risk of needing care is very high. Who needs to plan ahead for the payment of their care? Generally speaking, it is people who are moderately successful financially—people who will have estates between $200,000 and $2,000,000 in today's dollars at retirement. In other words, they have some money that's worth protecting, and the means to protect it, but they're not so wealthy that they can be completely independent of the need to plan ahead.

RISK DIAGRAM

91% chance that one spouse or the other will need Long-Term Care (average duration about 3 years)

79% chance that a 65 year old woman will need Long-Term Care (average female duration is 3.7 years)

58% chance that a 65 year old man will need Long-Term Care (average male duration is 2.2 years)

45% chance that both spouses will need Long-Term Care

The life expectancy for a 65 year old is nearly age 84. You're likely have a long road ahead-plan carefully!

40 percent of care in the U.S. is received by people under the age of 65.

3

The Cost and Types of Long-Term Care

The cost of Long-Term Care varies greatly across the U.S. According to Genworth's interactive Cost of Care map, the average 2012 cost for a private room in a nursing home in Oregon is about $85,000 per year. In Oklahoma, the cost is about $53,000 a year. In Connecticut, it's $140,000 a year. The cost of care is truly all over the map.[7]

In planning for care, consider where you plan to retire, and plan for the cost in that area rather than where you reside right now.

The Genworth map allows you to click on your state and then select specific areas within your state. It is updated each year. You should budget for the cost of a private room. You don't want a semi-private room if you can help it. Think of it this way: Your existing home may have multiple bathrooms, bedrooms, kitchen, living room, family room, etc. Imagine shrinking all those spaces down to one room-a bedroom/living room. That's a private room. Now imagine adding a roommate to that space. That's a semi-private room.

Most people would prefer to receive care at home. You'll find home care costs on the Genworth map as well.[8]

Each state has its own rules for licensing workers and facilities, and the definitions for "residential care," "assisted living," etc., can vary. Let's do an overview of the various levels of care from least to greatest. Their costs vary but the types of care are mostly similar across the country. These costs are for Oregon in 2012, courtesy of a survey by Gateway Living in Springfield, Oregon.

IN-HOME CARE

Private caregiver. Private caregivers often do light housekeeping, prepare meals, shop and run errands, coordinate transportation and social companion assistance, and provide light care, including personal hygiene, dressing, bathing assistance, and medication management. The costs are generally $14 to $20 per hour with a three-hour minimum per day.

Agency caregivers. Agencies provide caregivers who may be certified nurse's aides, licensed practical nurses, or even registered nurses. In addition to providing the same services as private caregivers, these licensed professionals can usually provide medication management and perform injections, skin integrity treatments, and wound care. They can also offer nursing assessments and coordinate with doctors for complicated treatment needs, such as dialysis, paralysis, and catheter and ostomy services. The costs range from $19 to $21 per hour for workers with the lowest level of licensure and from $25 to $40 per hour for registered nurses. Agencies often require a minimum of three hours of care per day and ten hours per week.

Ten hours of care per week will cost your family from $800 to $1,600 per month.

Medicare (Federal funding) *cannot* be used to pay for private or agency in-home care.

ADULT FOSTER HOMES

Adult foster homes (AFHs) are scattered throughout neighborhoods around the community and can have up to five adults living in one house. Care options vary and utilize a system of levels. Level I is the lowest level of care, level II is a moderate level of care, and level III is the highest level of care. Residents at level III have very few options: there aren't many AFH's that can handle residents with level III needs.

Owners of AFHs either provide care themselves, or they provide hired help at all times and manage the home personally. Often the AFH is not able to provide care throughout the night, when the hired caregivers are sleeping. At night, the caregivers are available for emergencies only. Depending on the level of care the house provides, one caregiver is usually delegated to provide housekeeping, caregiving, medication management, and meal service. Most AFHs are unable to provide memory-care services or dementia/Alzheimer's services. AFHs generally provide few activities; most residents tend to be private and watch television, read, or nap most of the day unless their family and friends provide social stimuli.

Costs. Level I homes charge between $1,650 and $2,500 per month. A level II or III home can range from $1,800 to $3,500 or more per month.

RETIREMENT RESIDENCES

These residences often feel like hotels, with studios, one-bedroom, and two-bedroom apartments that include a kitchenette, a small living and dining area, and a bathroom. These are ideal for active seniors who can care for themselves but appreciate the options of meal service (restaurant style), transportation to shopping centers and medical appointments, and a diverse selection of social activities.

When residents' needs for care services increase, they can hire caregivers, hire an agency to provide caregivers, or move to a facility that offers a higher level of care.

Costs. Retirement residences usually charge $1,800 to $3,400 per month. Housekeeping and laundry services are often available for an extra fee.

ASSISTED LIVING FACILITIES

Like retirement residences, assisted living facilities (ALFs) often feel like hotels with studios, one-bedroom, and two-bedroom apartments that include a kitchenette, a small living and dining area, and a bathroom.

Residents of ALFs can be somewhat independent but may need assistance with medications, meals, and activities. ALFs often provide many activities and can transport residents to shopping centers and doctor appointments. Card games, social outings, music groups, and of course, bingo are common.

The level of care (and associated costs) can vary according to the ratio of residents to caregivers. Most ALFs have a registered nurse (RN) on staff between 25 and 40 hours a week. The RN directs staff members as they manage certain tasks, such as administering medications. RNs can assess residents' needs in their homes, and then staff members can fax or call doctors to determine if the number of residents' doctor appointments can be reduced.

The ratio of caregivers to residents varies per shift, and some residents need assistance with most of the activities of daily living, so those residents are often assessed extra fees on a point scale.

Costs. ALFs charge between $2,200 and $4,500 per month. The more independent residents are, the less they are charged. These costs can vary from month to month as the residents' desires and needs fluctuate.

RESIDENTIAL CARE FACILITIES

Residential care facilities (RCFs) are often cottages in residential areas and retain some similarities to the residents' home: a smaller environment, one floor, and fewer residents. RCFs have a higher ratio of staff to residents, which means the staff members can provide a higher amount of care. The facilities can be either non-secured (residential) or secured (memory care) units. Memory-care units provide more staff and more security (such as a locked gate or door with a numerical code). Of course, memory-care units are more expensive than residential units.

All RCFs employ a licensed RN for at least 40 hours per week. The RN delegates certain tasks to the caregiving staff, such as administering medications. RNs can assess residents' needs in their homes, and then staff members can fax or call doctors to determine whether the number of residents' doctor appointments can be reduced.

RCFs generally look like a large home with up to 15 resident rooms, a dining room, a living room or common area, and an activity room. Most of the residents' rooms have a sink, a closet, and space for a bed, dresser, nightstand, and recliner. Bathrooms are sometimes shared by the residents on either side. Alternatively, the RCF will have two or three bathrooms for up to 15 residents.

Memory-care units and residential units may have differing activity calendars. Activities in residential units may be similar to those in assisted living facilities, whereas memory-care units offer activities that are less physically demanding.

Costs. Non-secured (residential care) units charge between $2,500 and $3,600 per month. They generally have a base rate for room and board and additional service fees for assistance needs. Secured (memory care) units charge from $3,700 to $4,800 per month. Many facilities are moving to a standard fee that encompasses all the levels of care (about $4,600), but some facilities still base charges on individual need.

REHABILITATION FACILITIES: SKILLED NURSING FACILITIES (SNFS), INTERMEDIATE CARE FACILITIES (ICFS)

These facilities used to be called nursing homes. They have come a long way in providing quality medical care in an institutional setting. Many facilities can accommodate 60 or even 90 residents (formerly called patients) and are mandated by the state to provide licensed staff for all levels of care. The residents generally require rehabilitation therapies (for example, after surgeries or injuries). Those who live in the intermediate level have acute medical needs, or they have gastro-intestinal tubes or IV therapy.

SNF and rehabilitation residents must be utilizing the therapy services available, which are overseen and authorized by Medicare or private insurance companies. Residents generally receive these services daily or at least five days per week in order to qualify for insurance benefits. The goal is to rehabilitate residents back to their baseline potential and enable them to maintain that in their next living situation or placement.

ICFs provide an intermediate level of care, usually for Long-Term residents who need 24-hour nursing services. Residents who have completed therapy programs in rehabilitation facilities may stay in ICFs (also called Long-Term sections) until they are placed in more permanent situations. The state regulates these facilities closely, and residents who require less care are transitioned to lower, more cost effective, and less institutional levels of care, such as memory care units, residential care facilities, or assisted living facilities.

Costs. These facilities charge between $6,500 and $8,500 per month.

CONTINUING CARE RETIREMENT COMMUNITIES

Continuing Care Retirement Communities, (CCRCs) are different from all the prior described care settings. They usually combine retirement living, assisted living, memory care, and rehabilitation facilities at one location. The idea is that you can move one last time, to a place which provides continuous care the remainder of your life, regardless of your physical condition. Normally you pre-fund your golden years in the CCRC with a single lump sum, but some will take a smaller lump sum up front and charge monthly rent.

COUNTING THE COST: IS IT REALLY THAT BAD?

$8,500 per month in a nursing home equates to over $100,000 per year. For the average woman who will require 3.7 years of care, that would be $370,000 in today's dollars! But even a private room in a skilled nursing facility or intermediate care facility is less expensive than 24/7 in-home care, which usually requires three people rotating eight-hour shifts every weekday—in addition to help for the weekend.

If all these costs sound like bad news, check out "Long-Term Care: What Are the Real Risks?"[8] This is an excellent *CBS Moneywatch* article by Steve Vernon. He points out that not all care costs $100,000 a year. Most people need a very low level of Long-Term Care at first and the need for care gradually increases as time goes by. If you asked me for a practical/logical guideline, I would tell you that I generally recommend planning (separately from savings and other assets) for two or three years of care per spouse (three or four years for single people) at 70-80 percent of the cost of a local skilled nursing facility (nursing home) in today's' dollars. In my local area, that amount would be about $320,000 per married couple, *minimum*. Here's the math: $100,000 (private nursing home room) x 80% x 2 (years) x 2 (partners in a marriage). $100,000 x 80% x 2 x 2 = $320,000.

These dollars need to keep pace with inflation. Later, I'll explain how a

2-3 year Long-Term Care Insurance benefit can often be leveraged to pay for five or more years of care.

Of course, accidents and catastrophic medical events can suddenly occur, requiring immediate, expensive Long-Term Care-and only you can decide whether you want to prepare financially for 15 years of care for dementia, ALS, or MS.

What if your money runs out in three years, but you still need care in a facility? Sarah Berkana of Gateway Living provides this answer.

> If the facility is licensed under both Medicare and Medicaid, i.e. "dual certified," and if the facility and the family agree on the length of private payments or Long-Term Care Insurance payments (usually between nine months and two years), *the resident can usually stay in the facility after depleting personal or insurance funds.* The facility may choose to move residents to smaller rooms or semiprivate (shared) rooms when they become Medicaid eligible, but not all facilities do. Families and residents should communicate their expectations and desires to the facility before admission to avoid surprises down the road. Residents and the facility will both be happier with that transparency.

4

Sources of Payment:
Who Pays for Care?

n broad terms there are only three sources which pay for Long-Term Care:

- the government
- your personal cash and assets
- insurance

This chart from the Kaiser Family Foundation shows the percentage each of these sources paid for Long-Term Care in 2010.[9]

Long-Term Care Financing

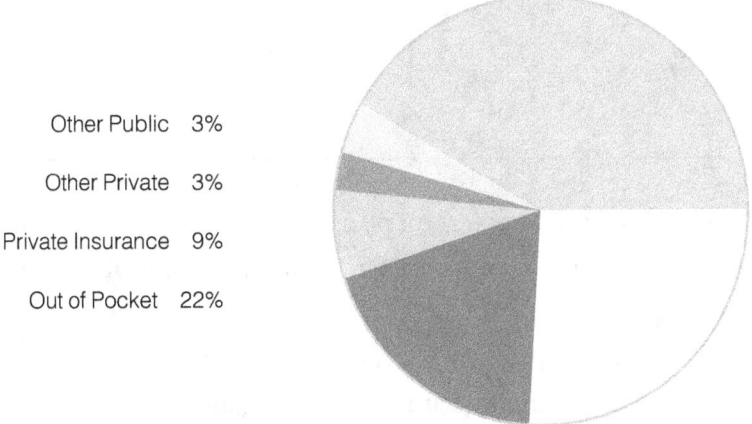

Other Public   3%

Other Private   3%

Private Insurance   9%

Out of Pocket   22%

Medicaid   40%

Medicare Post-Acute   23%

Long-Term Care Service	Medicare	Private Medigap Insurance	Medicaid	You Pay on Your Own
Nursing Home Care	Pays in full for days 0-20 if you are in a Skilled Nursing Facility following a recent hospital stay. If your need for skilled care continues, may pay for the difference between the total daily cost and your co-payment of $137.50/day for days 21-100. After day 100 does not pay.	May cover the $137.50/day co-payment if your nursing home stay meets all other Medicare requirements.	May pay for care in a Medicaid-certified nursing home if you meet functional and financial eligibility criteria.	If you need only personal or supervisory care in a nursing home and/ or have not had a prior hospital stay, or if you choose a nursing home that does not participate in Medicaid or is not Medicare-certified.
Assisted Living Facility (and similar facility options)	Does not pay	Does not pay	In some states, may pay care-related costs, but not room and board	You pay on your own except as noted under Medicaid if eligible.
Continuing Care Retirement Community	Does not pay	Does not pay	Does not pay	You pay on your own
Adult Day Services	Not covered	Not Covered	Varies by state, financial and functional eligibility required	You pay on your own [except as noted under Medicaid if eligible.]
Home Health Care	Limited to reasonable, necessary part-time or intermittent skilled nursing care and home health aide services, and some therapies that are ordered by your doctor and provided by Medicare-certified home health agency. Does not pay for on-going personal care or custodial care needs only (help with activities of daily living)[10]	Not covered	Pay for, but states have option to limit some services, such as therapy	You pay on your own for personal or custodial care, except as noted under Medicaid, if you are eligible.

This table shows that Medicare or Medigap/Medicare supplement plans provide little-to-no coverage for Long-Term Care. The same is true for health insurance for those under age 65. According to the table, you can pay for care yourself, or if you are impoverished, Medicaid may pay.

Next we'll start listing and explaining the sources of payment for Long-Term Care.

We'll start with government sources of payment, beginning with Medicaid because it pays for more care than any other source.

MEDICAID

Should you rely on Medicaid? Medicaid is welfare. Before it helps pay for care, you'll lose all your assets worth over $2000 not including your primary residence (if married), and you'll devote nearly 100% of your income to your own care.

Medicaid is a cooperative program funded by state and Federal tax-dollars, and administered by the states. The Federal government establishes the minimum benefits that must be offered, and each state has the option of expanding those benefits. If the state wishes to reduce or change the benefits, it must first obtain a Federal Medicaid waiver.

In 2010, Medicaid paid for 40% of all care nationwide (see previous chart). In 2005, it paid for 48.9%. You see the trend… Medicaid pays only when you can't afford care yourself. All the people who collect from Medicaid either were impoverished when they first needed care, or they spent some or all their money on Long-Term Care (the 22% on the previous chart) and then turned to Medicaid.

Remember, Medicaid benefits are not based on *needs*, they are based on *budgets*!

The Kaiser Family Foundation provides an excellent review of Medicaid benefits in each state.[9]

Medicaid is a means-tested program, meaning you must meet rigorous income and asset limits in order to qualify for benefits. If you think you can give away your money in order to qualify for Medicaid benefits, think again! Call an elder law or Medicaid attorney before going down that road. You'll save yourself a lot of heartache.

Speaking in very broad terms for married couples, both spouses' assets are aggregated together for determining eligibility. Your house, its contents, and your car are excluded from your assets when determining eligibility. You can have up to about $2,000 in a checking account or other liquid cash assets.

Next, your income is considered. Medicaid will not pay for care if you receive income of more than (approximately) $2,000 per month. In order to receive benefits from Medicaid, first nearly all your income must be assigned to a Long-Term Care facility. You're allowed to keep between $30 and $156 per month of your income for personal use, and if you're eligible the state will pay the balance of the cost of care.

The bottom line is that Medicaid is meant to be a resource for impoverished people. Your best strategy is to avoid depending on Medicaid. The government has been steadily closing loopholes that in the past have allowed people with assets to collect benefits. If Medicaid does pay for care on your behalf, you can consider the amount paid as an "interest free loan" to your estate. Medicaid will come back after its money after you pass away! This includes selling your home (if your spouse is still residing there, they'll wait until he/she passes away), all the furnishings within it, wedding rings, cleaning out your checking account, etc. At the point Medicaid pays for your care, you are a ward of the state, and no longer in control of your destiny.

MEDICARE

Medicare is health insurance for people age 65 and older, or who are under 65 but are on Social Security disability.

People often assume that Medicare will pay for Long-Term Care. But Medicare pays for care only if you're recuperating after a hospital stay covering at least three midnights and only for a maximum total of 100 days following that stay (and there are other restrictions to this benefit). Thus the 23% "Post-Acute" care in the previous chart represents a lot of short-term, very expensive recuperation following surgery, typically inside a skilled nursing facility. One could argue that Medicare does not pay for Long-Term Care at all, since Long-Term Care is generally defined as lasting a minimum of 90 days and Medicare is capped, per event, at a maximum of 100 days.

Bottom line: Medicare is health insurance, not Long-Term Care Insurance. If you are indeed recovering from a qualified surgery or hospital stay, Medicare will help pay for medical bills, physical and occupational therapy, and so on while you are recovering. But if your recovery "stalls," you have transitioned from needing medical care to needing Long-Term Care. Long-Term Care is for people who need *palliative* care (that is, care that reduces the pain or symptoms caused by their medical condition, rather than care which nurses them back to health) to maintain their current lifestyle or level of health, as well as for people whose health is worsening.

If you haven't recovered within 100 days following a hospital stay, Medicare will revert to simply paying medical bills. The physical and occupational therapy will be discontinued. I've spoken to a woman who is in charge of limiting the number of days a person is eligible for skilled nursing benefits following hospital stays, and she said it is a very, very difficult situation for all concerned. They will get you back home and out of skilled care as soon as humanly possible. Sometimes, however, people are released from skilled care directly into a nursing home.

VETERAN'S ADMINISTRATION (VA)

Two divisions of the VA are involved in Long-Term Care: Veterans Health Administration (VHA) and Veterans Benefits Administration (VBA). VHA runs all the VA health-care facilities and administers direct Long-Term Care benefits.

The VHA Long-Term Care benefits are very difficult to qualify for and extremely limited. They may help pay for facility care.

The VBA benefits are much broader, and if you are a veteran or spouse, you should check out this division. This benefit is called "aid and assistance," and to be eligible you must meet requirements in these five areas:

1. Wartime era service

2. Assets below $80,000, not counting the primary residence

3. Family income limits

4. Medical need of claimant

5. Family medical expenses

To collect benefits before you turn 65, you must have a service-related disability. Over age 65, disability is presumed.

VBA eligibility is similar to Medicaid eligibility, but it offers you more dignity, choices, and autonomy: a check arrives each month as a supplemental pension benefit, and you decide how to spend it. The range of this benefit is approximately between $1,000 and $2,000 per month.

This is a complex program. For more information, contact the U.S. Department of Veterans Affairs, or your state VA office.[11]

CASH AND ASSETS

This category may include many more options than you think. The first source of payment is your current income. If that is not adequate, the next source you would likely turn to would probably be your checking or savings accounts and CDs, followed by your IRAs, 401(k)s, and annuities.

Next, you might sell your real estate. Using real property to pay for Long-Term Care is risky because you don't know what it will be worth at the time you need to convert it to cash. You'd first want to use cash, CDs, annuities, and the like to pay for care, rather than real estate. (However, a reverse mortgage on your personal primary residence may be a good option. I'll explain that in a bit.) When we review hybrid Long-Term Care life and annuity products, you'll see that leveraging your cash to your benefit may be more effective than depending on your real estate. For now, just note that "hybrid" simply means insurance that serves more than one purpose: it serves its traditional function and it helps pay for Long-Term Care.

You may have another asset which you wouldn't normally think of in this context: life insurance (and not just the cash value). Later I'll discuss modern life insurance and how some new policies can be used to fund Long-Term Care. There are two ways to use existing policies to fund care while you're still living, however.

LIFE SETTLEMENTS AND VIATICAL SETTLEMENTS.

With a life settlement, you raise cash by selling your life insurance policy for its present value. This option is usually available only to women age 74 and older and to men age 70 and older. A viatical settlement is similar but is available only if you are terminally ill. These settlements do not usually apply to term life insurance; they're generally for permanent or whole-life insurance. If your life expectancy is short enough and you're old enough, your policy may be worth as much as 80 percent of its face value. This money is paid to you while you are living, to do with as you wish. No strings are attached.

In both options, someone buys your life insurance policy from you and makes a return on this investment when you die. The sooner you die, the greater their return. Some people find these options distasteful, but they do have a place and may help in time of need.

REVERSE MORTGAGES

Are you at least 62 years old? Will your house be paid off, or mostly paid off, when you retire? These are a couple of things to consider as you read about reverse mortgages.

Have you ever thought of a reverse mortgage as a last resort for impoverished people who have no assets or income besides their home? I once thought of reverse mortgages that way, but I was wrong.

A reverse mortgage can actually be a helpful tool to make your life more comfortable in retirement by improving your cash flow, and it may have a place in your Long-Term Care planning. I'll briefly review the *current* requirements to qualify and then give a couple of hypothetical uses. These requirements and parameters are subject to change at any time!

To be eligible for a reverse mortgage…

- You must be 62 or older.

- The mortgage must be on your principal residence.

- Single-family homes qualify-even up to four units.

- You *can* have an existing mortgage.

You can receive the funds in several ways:

- a one-time lump sum

- a line of credit

- monthly payments

- a combination of the above

There are quite a few myths about reverse mortgages. Contrary to what you may have heard…

- You *do* retain the title to your home.

- Any equity remaining at death goes to your heirs or estate. The bank does *not* keep the equity.

- Regarding loan repayment, reverse mortgages are *non-recourse* loans. If the value of your home is less than the bank has paid you, or if the amount the bank has paid you (plus interest) becomes greater than the value of your house, you are held harmless. You can stay in your house (as long as it is your primary residence) and do not have to repay the bank.

For example, let's say a 75-year-old couple wants to relocate. They sell their paid-for home for $400,000 and buy a new $400,000 home in another state. The traditional way to do this was to sell the old house and pay cash for the new house. The new way is to take out a reverse mortgage on the new house. The couple decides to take a lump sum. They pay $154,089 down and receive a lump sum of $249,911. Whether by the old way or the new way, they have no mortgage payment. But with the new way, they have $249,911 in their pockets.

Another example. A 74-year-old man wants to downsize. He sells his home for $400,000. He finds a new home for $250,000 and qualifies for a reverse mortgage. His down payment is $97,276, and $302,724 goes into his savings account. He has no mortgage payment.[12]

You can use a reverse mortgage to pay off your existing mortgage, which eliminates your payment and starts funds coming toward you rather than away from you. Or you can use a reverse mortgage to pay for Long-Term Care Insurance or other insurance products. You can even put cash in your pocket. There is a string attached, however: you cannot use the funds for investing. You must not place this principal at risk.

For more information about reverse mortgages, call a mortgage professional, such as a local member of the National Reverse Mortgage Lenders Association.[13]

5

Federal and State Incentives Related to Long-Term Care Insurance

There are several major pieces of Federal and state legislation which incentivize you to buy Long-Term Care Insurance or the new hybrid products. We'll review these prior to getting into the insurance itself.

Does it seem odd to you that Uncle Sam and your state government encourage you to buy private insurance? Medicaid budgets are being cut and the state and Federal governments are very interested in maintaining solvency. *You need to plan on paying for your own care.*

HEALTH INSURANCE PRIVACY AND PORTABILITY ACCOUNTABILITY ACT OF 1996 (HIPAA)

This privacy act is the reason we receive all those little booklets from various companies explaining how they're protecting our privacy. Part of the act created tax-qualified (TQ) Long-Term Care Insurance. If you buy tax qualified Long-Term Care Insurance, a portion of the premium qualifies as a medical expense toward a Federal tax deduction. Here are the limits on tax deductibility for tax qualified policies in 2013:

AGE	MAXIMUM DEDUCTION
40 or younger	$360
41–50	$680
51–60	$1,360
61–70	$3,640
71 or older	$4,550

Tax qualified policies have another advantage which I believe is more important than the tax benefit: they have a set of common standards. This makes shopping & comparing various plans from sundry companies a little easier. Although non-tax qualified policies are still available, this book specifically pertains to tax qualified policies. There are two primary similarities between the tax qualified policies from various insurers.

First, in order for you to qualify to receive benefits from a tax qualified contract, your doctor must confirm that you'll need help with two or more activities of daily living (ADLs) for 90 days or longer, or that you require assistance due to a cognitive impairment, such as dementia. You must have an approved plan of care and meet a couple of other requirements. (As a reminder, the physical ADLs are bathing, dressing, transferring [getting from a bed to a chair], toileting, eating, and continence.)

Second, the benefits are not taxable (in nearly all cases), and the premium may be deductible, as shown in the prior table.

In addition, most tax qualified policies are comprehensive. This generally means they cover care at home as well as in the community at facilities, and they must cover personal care, homemaker services, physical therapy, and skilled nursing care. Generally, services are considered *skilled* or *non-skilled* depending on the amount of training the service providers must have. Non-skilled services include cooking, cleaning, laundry, and the like. Skilled services include physical therapy, nursing care, and so on. There are some policies which only cover assisted living, or nursing homes, or only cover Long-Term Care following a hospital stay. These were mostly sold 15+ years ago, but there are still some out there. Some families have been burned by these older policies, leaving a bad taste in their mouth about Long-Term Care Insurance in general. It's no longer the Wild West of Long-Term Care Insurance of the 1980's and 1990's. It's safer now. Another reason to buy tax qualified Long-Term Care Insurance is that only tax qualified policies are eligible for Partnership benefits.

DEFICIT REDUCTION ACT OF 2005 (DRA)

This act created the option for states to join in a Partnership with the Federal government. Nearly 40 states now belong to this Partnership. The Partnership encourages the purchase of less expensive, limited-duration Long-Term Care Insurance policies by creating a Medicaid exclusion to one's estate.

In the past, many people purchased Long-Term Care Insurance with unlimited lifetime benefits in an attempt to avoid having Medicaid ever pay for nursing home bills on their behalf. Purchasing Long-Term Care

Insurance with unlimited lifetime benefits is very expensive. The Partnership creates some protection for one's estate from Medicaid, even with limited-duration policies.

Let's say Medicaid is paying for the care of one spouse in a nursing home while the other spouse remains at home. Upon the death of the second spouse, Medicaid has a claim to the value of the house/estate, up to the amount of care paid on behalf of each spouse. (If you're single, you lose the house prior to receiving benefits from Medicaid). The Partnership says that the portion of your estate equal to the benefits paid by your insurance policy. is excluded from being claimed by Medicaid, if you have received benefits from a Partnership qualified, Long-Term Care Insurance policy. Depending on your state of residence, you may have dollar-for-dollar estate protection, or 50 cents on the dollar. (Your state *may* limit the exclusion).

There is no additional charge for purchasing a Partnership policy, and the insurance coverage and policy are no different if they qualify as QPP's (Qualified Partnership Policies). It's not the insurance company that gives Partnership benefits; it's the state and Federal governments via the Medicaid exclusion. To obtain Partnership status, your plan must be Tax Qualified and have inflation protection as required by your state. We'll review inflation protection later, when discussing Long-Term Care Insurance.

There are two distinct benefits to a Partnership policy. *In addition to a measure of protection to your estate via the purchase of a Qualified Partnership Policy (QPP), you do not have to "spend down" your estate to prior to qualifying for Medicaid if you have a QPP.* Well run some numbers, but first I'll restate the benefit, as it is key to our discussion.

You might wonder why you would need a Medicaid exemption for your estate; after all, you purchased Long-Term Care Insurance in order to pay your own way, to avoid becoming impoverished and qualifying for Medicaid. Well, many people have seen high ($6,000 to $7,000 per year) Long-Term Care Insurance premiums, and have been discouraged or scared off. These high rates are typically for unlimited lifetime benefits. Policies which have a limited duration of 2-5 years are more affordable. The Partnership encourages you to buy a less expensive, limited policy, allowing you to protect *some* of your estate from being claimed after your death by Medicaid, rather than needing an unlimited lifetime Long-Term Care Insurance benefit to protect *most or all* of your estate in the case of a Long-Term Care event.

With a Partnership policy, if the policy benefits are exhausted, the state and Federal governments will back you up with Medicaid. The value of your policy is calculated by multiplying the daily or monthly benefit (monthly is better) by the duration of the policy. For example if you have a policy that pays $5,000 per month for five years/60 months, the value of that policy is $300,000.

In the above case, if you live in a state which offers dollar-for-dollar Partnership protection, you need to spend down your estate only until it is worth $300,000, prior to qualifying for Medicaid benefits (not considering income).

Or say you collect all $300,000 out of your policy, continue to need care, and run up a $500,000 bill with Medicaid. Because your Long-Term Care Insurance is Partnership qualified, Medicaid has to hold harmless the last $300,000 of your estate after you die. They can't claim it, so it goes to your heirs, charity, or wherever you want. This is a huge benefit, and it doesn't cost you a cent.[14] The deficit reduction act reopened the Partnership to new states starting in 2005. Now nearly 40 states have joined. There are four states that originally joined the Partnership when it was first created in the late 1980's. Their rules vary somewhat. The original states were California, Connecticut, Indiana, and New York.

PENSION PROTECTION ACT OF 2006 (PPA)

The PPA became effective January 1, 2010. It created tax-favored status for hybrid products. We'll talk more about hybrid products in a bit. Essentially, they leverage your money if you need Long-Term Care. For example if you pour $100,000 into a hybrid life-insurance plan, and that plan has an additional $300,000 Long-Term Care benefit, you've just quadrupled your money if you need Long-Term Care. Because of the PPA, you receive the extra $300,000 tax free if it is paid out for care. Hybrid products existed before the PPA, but the leveraged funds coming out were taxable.

Many states have tax deductions, and a few have tax credits as incentives for residents to purchase Long-Term Care Insurance. For example Maryland gives you a one-time $1,000 credit. 8-10 other states give an ongoing credit, and many other states give you an income tax deduction.[15] They really are anxious that you not burden the Medicaid system. Even in these tough economic times when state budgets are really stretched, I haven't heard of a single state rescinding these tax breaks.

THE CLASS ACT

The Community Living Assistance Services and Supports Act was part of President Obama's original health care reform bill. The CLASS Act was a federal Long-Term Care Insurance program. Coverage would be offered regardless of health, but benefits would not commence for 5 years after initial purchase of insurance. The Act was written so as to require that it "stand on its own two feet" financially. Eventually it was struck from the health care reform law, because even with 5 years premiums coming in before any claims would be paid, the actuaries couldn't make the numbers work.

The lesson here is that no matter how large a pool of potential insured's you're drawing from—even if it's the entire country, you can't have a solvent plan when anyone, regardless of health, can join in. This is a good time to talk about qualifying for insurance.

If you want Long-Term Care Insurance, do you qualify to purchase a policy? In general terms, you must be in good-to-fair health to purchase a policy. More specifically, it's not so much what your health history is, as much as the degree or severity of your existing conditions and/or the amount of recovery you've had from past conditions. For example I've placed policies on people who've had heart attacks, cancer, diabetes, stents, stenosis, joint replacements, and even strokes. To qualify for insurance, they'd either fully recovered from these issues, or the issues were ongoing but not severe.

If you don't qualify, you might see if something is available through your employer. Worksite LTC insurance often offers a 5-10% discount, and reduced health-underwriting to groups as small as three. Sometimes reduced underwriting is available for spouses. If you're in a position of authority at your place of business, you may want to install either an employee paid or employer-paid Long-Term Care Insurance plan. FYI Cafeteria plan dollars cannot be used to pay for this insurance on a pre-tax basis. HSA dollars can, within limits.

What does the future hold when it comes to medical underwriting? You can expect to see tighter health guidelines, and lower discounts for marital status or good health. Some of this has already happened.

You've seen that care is longer in duration for women, and therefore more expensive. Currently, Long-Term Care Insurance rates are unisex. In the future, expect to see higher rates for women than men. Expect to see more questions about family history, especially related to dementia & Alzheimer's. It is likely that genetic testing will become part of the underwriting process, as well as "insurance physicals" as with life insurance.

6

Long-Term Care Insurance

This is the granddaddy of insurance industry products when it comes to paying for Long-Term Care. The product was created for this sole purpose, but large premium quotes, rate increases, "gotchas," and other factors have scared many people off. The Federal and state government, financial advisors, CPA's etcetera, strongly recommend it, however, and its primary purpose is to pay for care - so let's take a look at it.

Like every other topic in this guide, you could easily attend a full day seminar to begin to get a handle on this product. There is no denying it is complex. Find someone who has the CLTC designation, is a member of AALTCI, and whom you feel has your best interests in mind if you choose to obtain quotes or compare policies.

We'll limit the discussion to Tax Qualified products, and we'll answer the seven most common questions people ask about Long-Term Care Insurance.

TOP SEVEN QUESTIONS ABOUT LONG-TERM CARE INSURANCE

1. What is the right age to buy?

2. How much does it cost?

3. Can I trust the insurance company to stand behind what they sell?

4. Will the company be able to pay benefits when I need them?

5. How do I choose a company?

6. What if my rates go up?

7. What if I pay 30 years and never need it or use it?

Let's start with the basics. When you design your plan, you are required to make only three decisions:

- How much will it pay, per day or month? (Monthly is better.)

- How long will it pay? (You choose the duration)

- When does it start paying? (You choose an elimination period. This is the time after you need care but before benefits begin. The most common elimination period is 90 days, which more or less fits with the lifetime Medicare benefit of 100 days. If you qualify to receive Medicare-paid Long-Term Care, those days of care generally count toward your elimination period).

When you purchase a modern Long-Term Care Insurance policy, you're purchasing access to a pool of money. You have immediate access to the entire pool of money from the effective date of your contract/policy. Most policies reimburse you for covered expenses after you've first paid for them. Some will give you cash in lieu of reimbursement, to use as you see fit as long as you qualify to receive benefits. For example you could use the cash to pay family members to provide care.

A typical pool of money might be $150,000 to $200,000 per person. In the hypothetical example below, one premium payment of $200 gives access to the entire pool of funds.

When you purchase Long-Term Care Insurance, you purchase access to a pool of money. You have immediate access to the entire pool of money from the effective date of your contract/policy.

Optional inflation protection will grow your pool over time.

A typical pool of money might be $150,000–$200,000 per person. Funds can be used for in-home care or facility care.

When you design your plan, you choose a maximum rate at which you can access funds for care.

Example: One premium payment of $200 gives you access to the entire pool of funds.

$200

Rule of thumb: a lifetime of premiums will never add up to more than the cost of one year in a nursing home.

There are many options for these plans, but let's keep it simple! You need only make three choices to design your plan:

- Maximum payout per month
- How long will it pay
- When does it start paying

> As a rule of thumb, a lifetime of premiums will never exceed the cost of one year in a nursing home.

Funds from a comprehensive policy can be used for in-home care or facility care. The pool of money is calculated by multiplying the monthly benefit by the duration of benefits you've chosen.

When you design your plan, you choose a maximum rate at which you can access funds for care. For example, you could buy a policy that will pay up to $3000/month for 72 months, or a policy that will pay up to $6000/month for 36 months. Each policy is worth $216,000, but the rate at which they will reimburse you for the cost of care is different. The first example above is what the industry calls a "long-thin" plan design, and the second is a "short-fat" plan. Short-fat plans cost more, but there are advantages which we'll review later.

Optional inflation protection will grow your pool over time. If you purchase a new tax qualified policy that meets your state's minimum inflation protection requirement for your age, and other Partnership requirements, a portion of your estate is exempt from being claimed by Medicaid after your death.

There are many riders, but only three that I generally recommend:

1. Inflation protection. This rider will typically comprise 40 to 60 percent of the total premium (See the following graph). To obtain Partnership protection in most states, here is the guideline: if you are age 60 or younger you need to purchase compound inflation protection. Age 61–75, any type of inflation protection is okay. If you're 75 or better there is not an inflation protection requirement. Inflation protection comes in many flavors. There is compound inflation protection, simple inflation protection, inflation protection based on the Consumer Price Index (CPI), etc.

2. Shared care for couples. If one spouse or partner exhausts his or her pool of funds, that person can then tap into the other's policy. This is available if the two policies are with the same company, issued at the same time with the same benefits. This adds approximately 20 to 25 percent to the premium. (Note that most companies will not let the spouse collecting benefits to actually drain the other spouses' policy totally dry).

3. Waiver of the home health-care elimination period. With this rider you'll have coverage from day one if you qualify to receive

home care. This rider typically adds 7-10% to your premium, although some plans have it automatically built in.

A note on the Shared Care rider: generally speaking, when you exhaust the benefits of your own policy, you begin tapping into your partner's pool of benefits. There are at least two exceptions to this type of Shared Care as of this writing. Policies from these two companies create a *separate*, third pool of benefits via the Shared Care rider. This is preferred because in essence you'll get 50% more coverage with these two carriers compared to the rest of the industry. Normally when you each purchase a 3 year benefit you get 3+3 = 6 years of total coverage. With these two companies, however, when

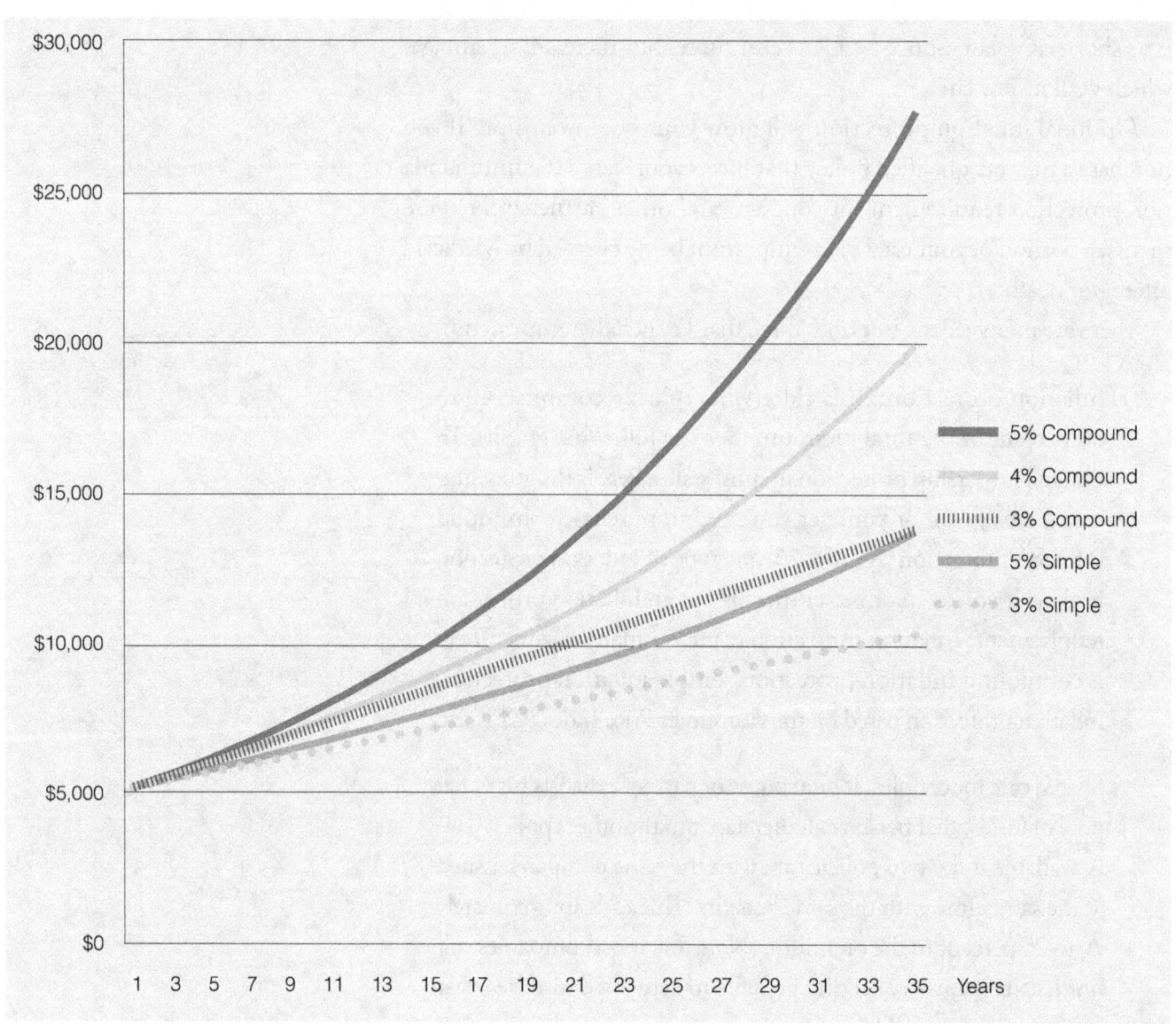

Why is inflation protection so expensive? This inflation graph shows that if you have 5% compound inflation protection, the insurance company will pay over 500% of your initial benefit, for a claim 35 years in the future! The growth and benefits are generally tax-free.

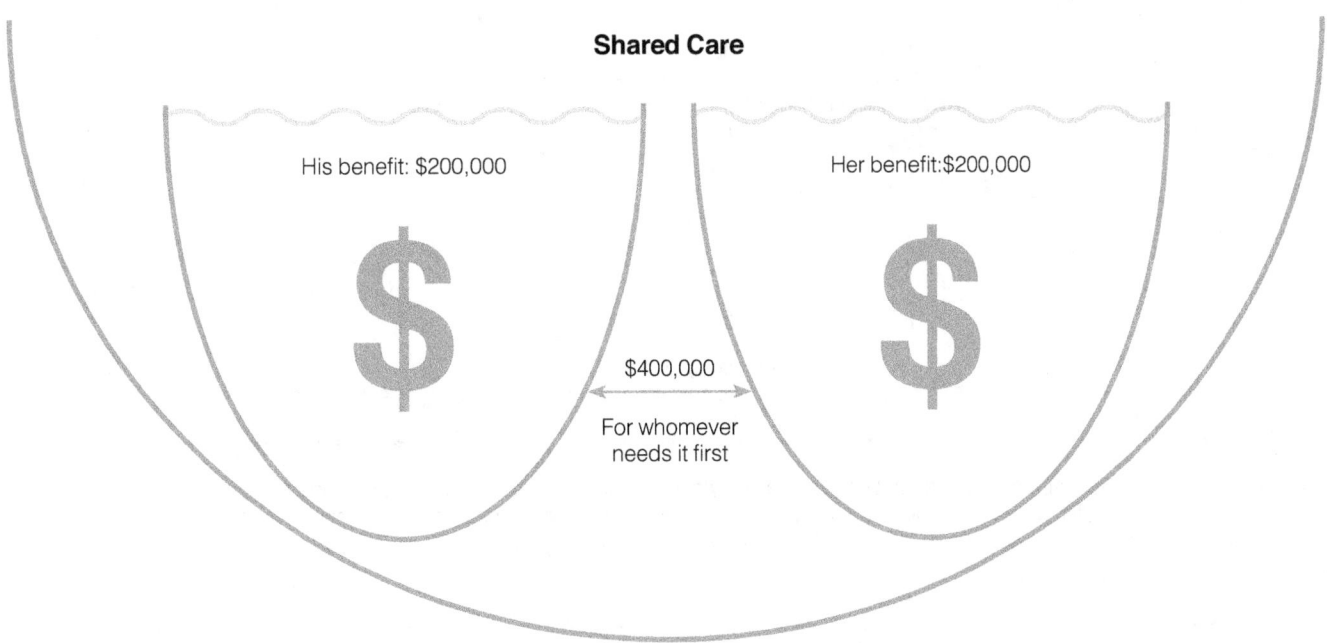

Shared Care

His benefit: $200,000

Her benefit:$200,000

$400,000

For whomever needs it first

> If you're married, you and your spouse can best leverage your premium and coverage via the "shared care" rider. The shared care rider allows one partner to tap into the other partners' pool of funds if they first exhaust their own. Shared care is generally available to partners as well as spouses.

you each buy a 3 year benefit, you get 3+3+3 years of benefits, for a total of 9. If one spouse needs 6 years of care there still remain 3 years for the other spouse, because with these two companies you aren't taking benefits from your spouse when you tap into the shared care benefit.

I've mentioned a *monthly* Long-Term Care Insurance benefit is preferable to a *daily* benefit. The reason has to do with home care, the type of care you're most likely to need. Let's say you purchase a $6000 per month benefit, which is the equivalent of $200 per day. Let's also say you eventually need home care, 10 hours per day, three days per week, at $30 per hour. $30 per hour at 10 hours per day means a bill to you of $300 per day. If you buy a $200 per day benefit, you'll be short by $100 per day and you'll have to pay cash for that extra $100-the insurance will only pay $200. But if you buy $6000 per month, all $300 per day is covered, up to 20 days per month. There isn't a daily limit, there is only a monthly limit. The companies which allow you to choose daily or monthly benefits will usually charge about 8% more for monthly benefits. Now you know why.

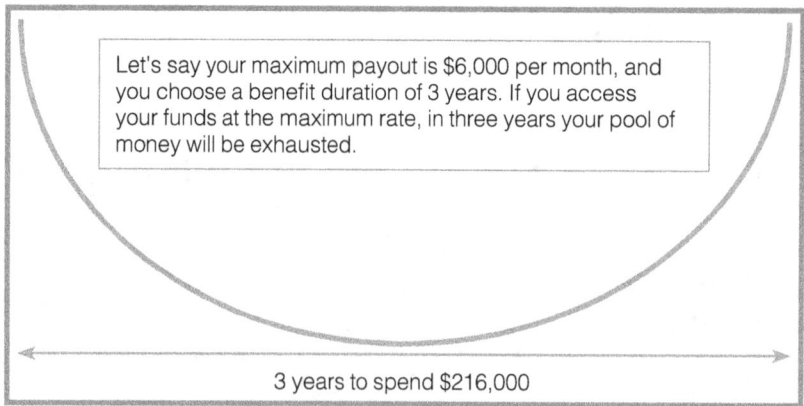

Let's say your maximum payout is $6,000 per month, and you choose a benefit duration of 3 years. If you access your funds at the maximum rate, in three years your pool of money will be exhausted.

3 years to spend $216,000

Same plan as above, but let's say you only need some in-home care or assisted living care, and it costs $3,000 per month. If you access your funds at a slower pace, your pool of money lasts longer. You are not "cut off" from benefits unless you spend every last cent in your pool.

6 years to spend $216,000

1. WHAT IS THE RIGHT AGE TO BUY LONG-TERM CARE INSURANCE?

Examples of the Cost of Long-Term Care Insurance			
Age at purchase (husband and wife at the same age)	50	60	70
Monthly benefit amount each (4 percent inflation, compound)	$5,000	*$7,500	*$11,000
Annual combined premium, both spouses	$2,360**	$4,564	$16,303
Cumulative premiums paid to age 80	$70,800	$91,200	$163,030
The additional premiums paid if you start later than age 50	$0	$20,400	$92,230

Assumptions: select rates, two-year duration (each), husband and wife both insured and the same age, with shared care. *Based on 4% compound inflation, the couple's original $5000 monthly benefit would grow to about $7500 in 10 years, and $11000 in 20 years.

**These rates include a 30 percent discount given when both spouses obtain for coverage. If you are single, your rate is approximately 72 percent of the combined total rate you see above for a couple.

Buying at a younger age will *always* save you money in the long run when you consider cumulative premiums to age 80 and beyond.

- Premiums are based on your age when you apply. The younger you are, the less costly your premiums will be. *Lower premiums will be easier to pay during retirement years.*

- Your eligibility and rate classification are based on your health when you apply. You're more likely to receive a "Preferred" discount (for being in exceptional health) of 10-15% if you apply younger, and that discount is good for life.

- The younger you are, the more likely you are to qualify for coverage. More than 45 percent of applicants over age 70 are refused coverage after applying, due to health problems.

- Insurance companies tend to close existing products, and offer new products about every three years to new customers, with rates that are 15 to 25 percent higher.

Here's a real-life quote from May 2012. The first column gives the title of each row. Columns 2-3 show the benefits & premiums for a husband and wife, and reflect a "marital discount." Column 4 is a quote for a single person. This table shows the impact on premium for a couple with the marital discount plus shared care rider, versus the premium rate for a single person.

2. HOW MUCH DOES IT COST?

AGE	60-APPLICANT ("STANDARD HEALTH" RATE)	60-PARTNER (PREFERRED HEALTH" DISCOUNT)	60-SINGLE
Facility Daily Benefit	$170	$170	$170
Facility Benefit Period	2 Year	2 Year	2 Year
Monthly Home Care	Yes	Yes	Yes
Inflation Protection	4%	4%	4%
Facility Elimination Period	90 Days	90 Days	90 Days
Shared Care Benefit	**Yes**	**Yes**	**No, N/A**
Marital Discount	Both Insured	Both Insured	None
Premium Mode	Monthly	Monthly	Monthly
Notes: Pool of money: $120,000, Cash Benefit: 40%, Rate Guarantee: 5 years			
Premium Per Person	$136.91	$116.37	
Total Monthly Premium	**$253.28**		**$181.57**

This quote looks similar to the prior one, but it has a different purpose. This shows husband & wife in columns 2-3 with inflation protection, and columns 4-5 without inflation protection. The benefits are identical the first year, but over time the added cost for inflation protection will be worthwhile, as benefits increase but premiums stay level.

AGE	60 APPLICANT ("STANDARD" RATE)	60 PARTNER (PREFERRED HEALTH" DISCOUNT)	60 APPLICANT ("STANDARD" RATE)	60 PARTNER (PREFERRED HEALTH" DISCOUNT)
Facility Daily Benefit	$170	$170	$170	$170
Facility Benefit Period	2 Year	2 Year	2 Year	2 Year
Monthly Home Care	Yes	Yes	Yes	Yes
Inflation Protection	**4%**	**4%**	**Optional**	**Optional**
Facility Elimination Period	90 Days	90 Days	90 Days	90 Days
Shared Care Benefit	Yes	Yes	Yes	Yes
Marital Discount	Both Insured	Both Insured	Both Insured	Both Insured
Premium Mode	Monthly	Monthly	Monthly	Monthly
Notes: Pool of money: $120,000, Cash Benefit: 40%, Rate Guarantee: 5 years				
Premium Per Person	$136.91	$116.37	$74.37	$63.22
Total Monthly Premium	**$253.28**		**$137.59**	

Can these companies be trusted? Your state insurance division may have some help for you on this topic. For example, Oregon offers a booklet called *Consumer Guide to Insurance Complaints.* This book ranks insurers based on written complaints filed against them. The ranks are standardized based on the size of the company. Complaints which are investigated and judged valid are included in the rankings. Your state insurance website may have similar information. These are the same insurance companies which operate in your state, so this data should be considered relevant regardless of your location.

The following table is from the 2012 Guide, with data from 2011.[16]

3. CAN I TRUST THE INSURANCE COMPANY TO STAND BEHIND WHAT THEY SELL?

Company Name	2011 Premium	Total Complaints	Confirmed Complaints	Complaint Index	2011 Ranking
Ability Ins. Co.	$4,400,358.00	1	0	0.00	3
Allianz Life Ins. Co. of North America	$2,560,161.00	0	0	0.00	7
Bankers Life and Casualty Co.	$13,167,829.00	17	17	4.48	19
Continental Casualty Co.	$8,985,056.00	8	4	1.55	16
Equitable Life and Casualty Ins. Co.	$5,756,360.00	9	2	1.21	15
Genworth Life Ins. Co.	$19,839,420.00	2	1	0.17	12
John Hancock Life Ins. Co.	$18,675,986.00	2	2	0.37	13
Lincoln Benefit Life Co.	$2,484,035.00	0	0	0.00	8
Metropolitan Life Ins. Co.	$6,263,981.00	2	2	1.11	14
Mutual of Omaha Ins. Co.	$1,606,472.00	0	0	0.00	10
New York Life Ins. Co.	$2,002,924.00	0	0	0.00	9
Northwestern Long Term Care Ins. Co.	$3,972,253.00	0	0	0.00	5
Prudential Insurance Co. of America	$2,671,382.00	0	0	0.00	6
Regence BlueCross BlueShield of Oregon	$1,255,623.00	0	0	0.00	11
RiverSource Life Ins. Co.	$3,384,538.00	2	2	2.05	18
State Farm Mutual Automobile Ins. Co.	$5,420,608.00	0	0	0.00	2
Thrivent Financial for Lutherans	$2,114,874.00	1	1	1.64	17
Transamerica Life Ins. Co.	$4,155,282.00	1	0	0.00	4
UNUM Life Ins. Co. of America	$11,613,643.00	0	0	0.00	1
Total for this table	**$120,330,785.00**	**45**	**31**		
Total for long-term care	**$131,883,174.00**	**59**	**38**		

That's 38 confirmed complaints on $131.9 million in premium. Nearly ½ of those complaints are against one insurer...draw your own conclusion about that company. Remove that company and you can see that the vast majority of policyholders are satisfied.

4. WILL THE COMPANY BE ABLE TO PAY BENEFITS WHEN I NEED THEM?

Long-Term Care Insurance companies are usually ranked by their Comdex ratings. The Comdex rating's, a "combined index" of the ratings from A.M. Best (statutory financial condition), Standard & Poor's (financial strength), Moody's (claims paying ability), Fitch Ratings (financial strength), and Weiss (financial strength). The companies are ranked by percentile against all life insurance companies in the U.S. Thus a rating of 90 means the company is reckoned to be stronger than 89 percent of all other life insurance companies in the U.S. Here are the Comdex ratings of some of the top companies currently selling new policies, as of February, 2012:

Genworth Life Insurance Co 79
Mutual & United of Omaha 91
John Hancock Life & Health Insurance 93
Transamerica Life Insurance 93

You might consider a mutual company. Mutual companies do not have stockholders and are not beholden to them. They are owned by their policyholders. Some believe that because they do not have stockholders and therefore aren't under pressure to show a certain level of profit, they may be less likely to raise rates. Met Life and Prudential are not listed above because they no longer sell new individual Long-Term Care Insurance policies. They will continue to service their existing books of business.

Most states have a guaranty fund, created by a premium tax paid by insurers to the states where they do business. Thus the insurance company's ability to pay claims may be backed up to an extent by the strength of your state.[17]

5. HOW DO I CHOOSE A COMPANY?

I recommend you look at several factors:

- Commitment to the market. Do you perceive that the company is here to stay?

- Financial strength ratings. Is the company strong enough for your comfort?

- Favorable underwriting. Does the company want your business, once they know your medical history? (Various medical conditions will result in different underwriting outcomes from one company to the next).

- Good customer service. The Consumer Complaint Guide, for example, helps you determine a company's service record.

- Price and value. Get several quotes for similar benefits, side by side. How do they stack up?

6. WHAT IF MY RATES GO UP?

The rates may go up. Long-Term Care Insurance is a form of health insurance-so it's likely your rates will go up at some point after purchase. If the rates do rise, it will be only if and when your state insurance commissioner allows them to. The insurance company must prove to the insurance commissioners' satisfaction that rates must rise in order for the insurer to remain fiscally sound. Still, the sooner you buy, the less you pay (based on your age and health at the time of purchase). Tax qualified policies also have a clause called contingent non-forfeiture. Under the right circumstances this clause allows you to decrease benefits as an alternative to avoid a large rate increase. In the end, if your insurance company proves to your insurance commissioners' satisfaction that the rate increase is needed and it is approved by your commissioner, you have the assurance of knowing that your benefits remain secure.

7. WHAT IF I PAY 30 YEARS AND NEVER NEED IT OR USE IT?

It's "pay as you go," like your auto insurance or homeowners' insurance policies. You have the coverage partly for peace of mind. If you didn't have a mortgage, wouldn't you still buy homeowners' insurance? The cost to repair damage is so large compared to the small premiums you pay in order to transfer that risk to the insurer. After age 65, your risk of a major house fire during your lifetime is less than 3 percent, but your risk of becoming physically or cognitively impaired is nearly 70 percent—over 23 times more likely.17 In large part, insurance rates are based on the likelihood that you'll need to place a claim on the policy benefits. Simply put, the reason Long-Term Care Insurance appears expensive, is that it is so likely that you'll collect benefits from your policy.

There is a *waiver of premium* benefit in tax qualified Long-Term Care Insurance: if you go on claim, the premiums stop for the duration of the claim. It's a very beneficial clause. If "what if I never need" it is an important issue to you, consider purchasing a rider called "enhanced non-forfeiture."

For an extra charge, this rider says that policy benefits will be paid if you need care, even after canceling your policy, if you first keep the policy a predetermined number of years. Some policies will refund premiums if you die under age 65 or 70 without ever having claimed on the policy. Other policies will refund all your premiums at age 90 or 95 if you have not claimed benefits, if you are still living; a "money-back guarantee."

Risk Of Various Events After Reaching Age 65[18]

Event	Risk
Risk of major house fire (men)*	2.2%
Risk of major house fire (women)*	2.6%
Risk of severe car accident (men)*	15.5%
Risk of severe car accident (women)*	18%
Risk of both spouses needing Long-Term Care (married couple)†	45%
Risk of needing Long-Term Care (men)‡	58%
Risk of needing Long-Term Care (women)‡	79%
Risk of one or the other spouse needing Long-Term Care (married couple)†	91%
Risk of death (regardless of gender)§	100%

0% 10% 20% 30% 40% 50% 60% 70% 80% 90% 100%

* according to the American Association for Long-Term Care Insurance, AALTCI.org

† according to an AARP study: http:www.aarp.org/relationships/caregiving/info2007/fs27r_ltc.html, and longtermcare.gov

† derived by applying a mathematical formula to ‡

§ same as taxes

7

Hybrid Insurance (Two Birds; One Stone)

Hybrid insurance" for our purposes simply means "one product that serves more than one function." These policies are also known as "linked-benefit," "combo" or "asset based" policies. Hybrid life insurance has a death benefit, as does traditional life insurance. It also provides a Long-Term Care benefit if needed, while you're living. Hybrid annuities can provide an income stream as can traditional annuities, but if you need Long-Term Care the payout is greatly increased.

Some people can afford Long-Term Care Insurance but don't want to pay the premiums year after year, or they mistrust the companies, or they feel the premiums are being wasted, etc. Hybrid products may answer these concerns.

The numbers used in these examples are real numbers from quotes obtained in May 2011.

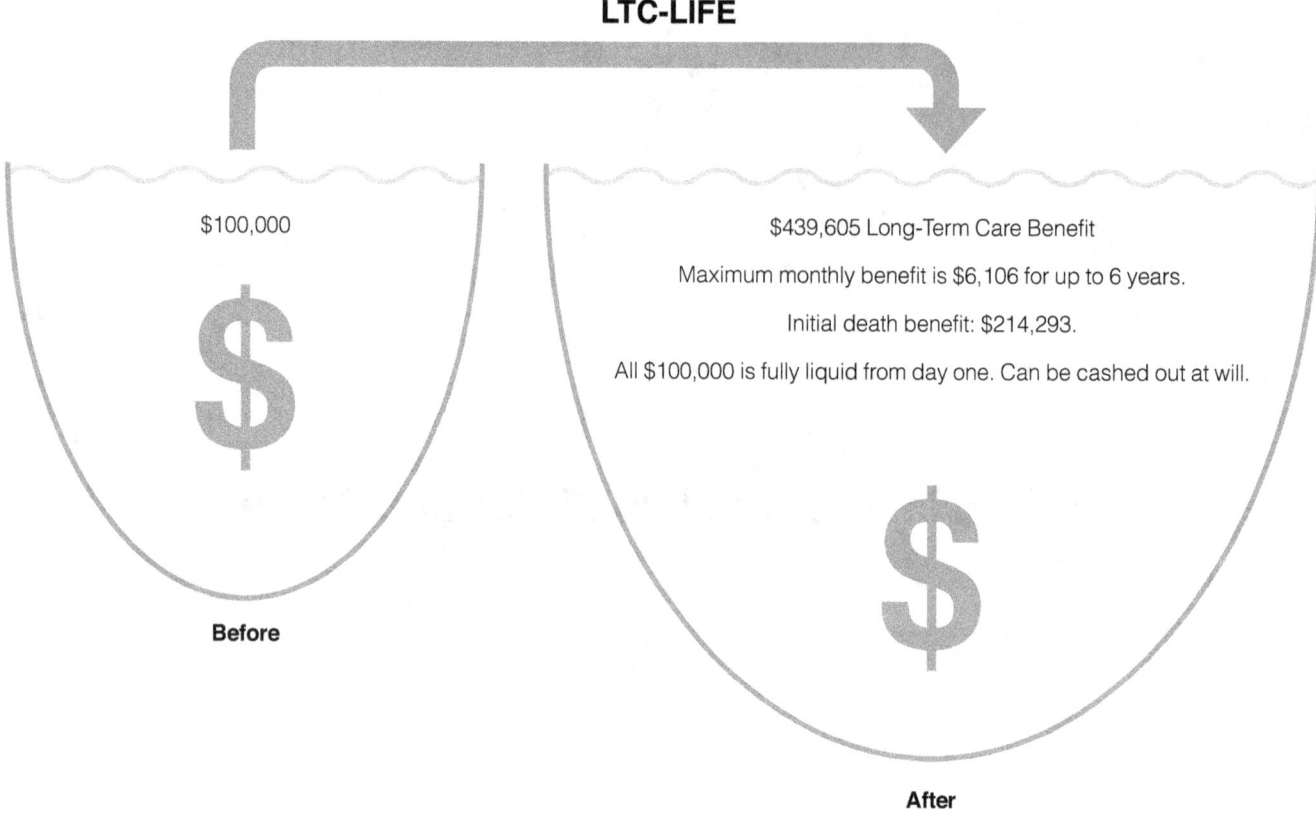

LTC-LIFE

$100,000

Before

$439,605 Long-Term Care Benefit

Maximum monthly benefit is $6,106 for up to 6 years.

Initial death benefit: $214,293.

All $100,000 is fully liquid from day one. Can be cashed out at will.

After

Long-term care life insurance. In this example a 65-year-old nonsmoking male pours $100,000 into the policy.

- He has several options for paying the premiums: from an existing life insurance policy, a CD, a checking account, a reverse mortgage, a 1035 exchange from an annuity, and so on.

- If he needs Long-Term Care, his money is worth nearly 4.4 times what he has paid into the policy. If he goes on claim, his money comes out first, then the insurance company's money. Because of the Pension Protection Act, the insurance company money comes out tax-free.

- The money he deposits is fully liquid. If he wants to take part of his initial deposit back out, the Long-Term Care benefit is decreased proportionally, but the policy continues.

- The Long-Term Care benefit with these policies can be structured in all sorts of ways. For example, he could deposit less money, but have the same monthly benefit with a shorter duration.

You can pull 100% of your initial premium deposit out anytime you want to. In that sense, the policy looks "free." The policy has a little life insurance and a lot of Long-Term Care Insurance benefits. Those benefits are paid for by the earnings the insurance company is making on the money you put in their custody. Right now that might only be 3 percent or so. Still, that's $3,000 per year that they're making on your money—and that you are *not* making on your money. This may be a good place to park some "rainy day, just in case" money, especially if you're older and the loss of the return on your $100,000 may be less important. If your money is in a checking or savings account earning 1 percent interest, you'll not lose much if you move the funds into this plan.

HYBRID LIFE INSURANCE VERSUS LONG-TERM CARE INSURANCE	
Advantages	**Disadvantages**
Your cash stays liquid and accessible. You are in control.	Your benefits do not grow over time to keep pace with inflation.
No ongoing premium payments.	Not Partnership qualified.
Life insurance benefit.	No tax credit or deduction.
The policy leaves something of value to your estate after your death.	These policies are generally for individuals and don't offer joint benefits for Long-Term Care. There is only one exception the author is aware of at this time; a joint-life policy which will pay benefits for either insured, making it somewhat equivalent to the "shared care" benefit of Long-Term Care Insurance on couples.
Possibly reduced underwriting. Some who don't qualify for Long-Term Care Insurance due to health reasons, may qualify for these policies.	
No ongoing premiums= no rate increases	

LTC-ANNUITY

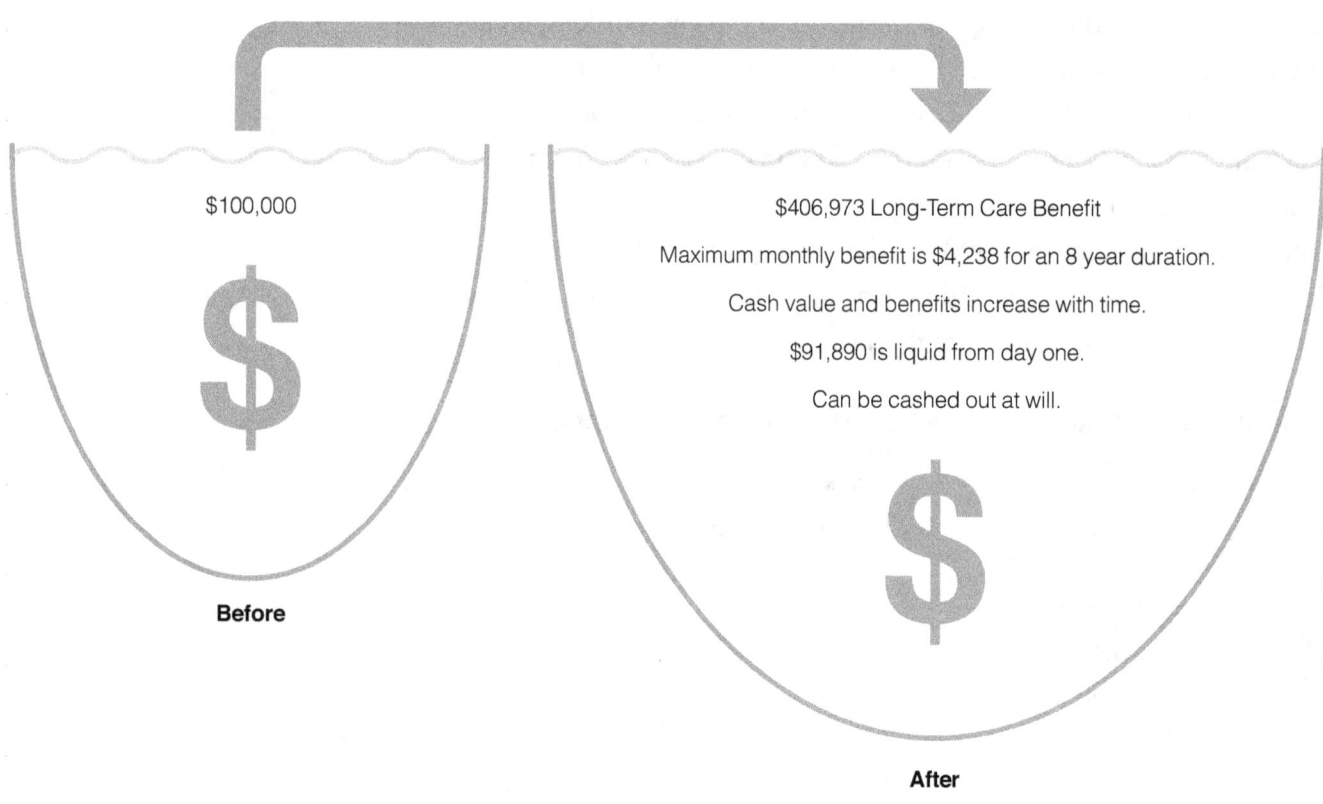

$100,000

Before

$406,973 Long-Term Care Benefit

Maximum monthly benefit is $4,238 for an 8 year duration.

Cash value and benefits increase with time.

$91,890 is liquid from day one.

Can be cashed out at will.

After

Long-Term Care Annuity. A 65 year old deposits $100,000 into the annuity policy.

- Her money can come from an existing life insurance policy, a CD, a checking account, a reverse mortgage, an existing annuity through a nontaxable 1035 exchange (non-qualified funds), and so on.

- If she needs Long-Term Care, her money is worth more than four times what she has poured into the policy. If she goes on claim, her money comes out first and then the insurance company's money. Because of the Pension Protection Act, the insurance money comes out tax-free.

- The money is mostly liquid. About $8,000 is held back if the policy is cancelled immediately. Over time, the funds become fully liquid. If she wants to take part of her money back out, the Long-Term Care benefit is decreased proportionally, but the policy continues.

- These policies can be structured in all sorts of ways. For example, he/she could put less money in but have the same monthly benefit with a shorter duration.

HYBRID ANNUITIES VERSUS LONG-TERM CARE INSURANCE	
Advantages	**Disadvantages**
Your cash stays mostly liquid and accessible.	Not Partnership qualified.
No ongoing premium payments.	No tax credit or deduction.
The policy leaves something of value to your estate after your death.	
Possibly reduced underwriting. Some who don't qualify for Long-Term Care Insurance due to health reasons, may qualify for these policies.	
Benefits increase over time based on the return on initial premium but will not generally keep pace with inflation. Still, your money grows, unlike LTC life insurance, where your initial policy value remains static over time.	
At least one hybrid annuity offers joint benefits, somewhat equivalent to the "shared care" benefit of Long-Term Care Insurance on couples.	

The Pension Protection Act took effect January 1, 2010. Since its passage, the leveraged dollars in a hybrid policy come out tax-free if used for Long-Term Care.

8

Other Insurance Which Helps Pay for Long-Term Care

S ome other products from the insurance industry can help with Long-Term Care but are not true hybrids.

IMPAIRED RISK IMMEDIATE ANNUITY

This annuity is underwritten for health conditions—the worse your health is, the better it pays! The income from an annuity is based on life expectancy. The older you are, the more you'll collect each month once you begin taking payments. To qualify for an impaired risk immediate annuity, you must be in very poor health or currently receiving care. Your annuity payments will increase as if you were older than you really are.

UNIQUE DEFERRED ANNUITY.

Deferred simply means you are deferring the payout to a later date of your choice, rather than taking income from the annuity when it is first purchased as with immediate annuities.

Of value when it comes to Long-Term Care, you can add a rider that doubles your income stream if you need Long-Term Care that fits the definition inside the policy (only facility care qualifies for benefits, not home care). You can add the rider as long as you're not receiving care at the time of purchase. As you'd expect, other restrictions may apply.

WHOLE LIFE & UNIVERSAL LIFE.

I mentioned earlier that some of the newer life insurance products are favorable toward Long-Term Care needs and offer living benefits to the policyholder. For example, the company I'm personally insured with offers two living riders: chronic illness (CI) and terminal illness (TI). These riders are free, and they're available only on whole-life products.

The chronic illness (Long-Term Care) rider pays out while you're living, much like Long-Term Care Insurance.

Your doctor must certify that for at least 90 consecutive days, you are unable to perform at least two ADLs without substantial assistance or that you suffer from cognitive impairment. There are limits to the payout, depending on your age, life expectancy, etc.

The terminal illness rider pays out while you're living if a physician has certified that your life expectancy is 24 months or less. The maximum living benefit is 50 percent of the full death benefit at that time or $500,000, whichever is smaller.

In the following example we have a 60-year-old woman, rated as a preferred nonsmoker, purchasing a $500,000 policy with a premium of $570 per month.

UNIVERSAL LIFE VERSUS LONG-TERM CARE INSURANCE	
Advantages	**Disadvantages**
If you die before age 120, a substantial benefit goes to your estate.	Not Partnership qualified.
Rates are guaranteed to never increase, up to age 120.	No tax credit or deduction.
	Does not increase in value over time, as does Long-Term Care Insurance with an inflation rider.

Universal Whole Life with Long-Term Care Rider

Premium is $570 per month

$500,000 Death Benefit, guaranteed until age 120.

If terminally ill, she can receive an advance of 50% or $250,000

If chronically ill & qualifying for LTC benefit, she can receive up to 24% per year or $120,000 per year.

Premium rates can't ever go up.

Term Life Insurance with Terminal Illness Rider

Premium is
$107 per month

$500,000 Death Benefit, guaranteed level for 10 years.

If terminally ill, she can receive an advance of 50% or $250,000

If chronically ill & qualifying for the LTC benefit,
she has the right to convert this policy *during the first 5 years*
and collect as in the prior visual illustration.

$

TERM LIFE INSURANCE

Several companies have riders that allow you to take advances on your whole-life or universal-life death benefit while you are living as described above. But to my knowledge, only one U.S. company allows you to purchase term insurance and accomplish the same result.

This company allows you to convert your term life insurance plan to a universal-life plan and add the chronic illness rider *during the first five years of the policy.* Other companies allow this, too-as long as your health is still good. The unique thing here is that this company allows you to add the CI rider even if you convert *after* needing Long-Term Care or becoming seriously ill or disabled. In other words, there is no underwriting for the chronic illness rider if you convert during the first five years of your policy

In this example, our 60-year-old woman purchases 10-year term insurance, qualifying for preferred nonsmoker rates, for $107 per month. During the first five years this policy can be converted to a universal life policy and then be used to pay for Long-Term Care if she qualifies for benefits under the rules of the chronic illness rider.

This option is an inexpensive way for people to get some protection. It allows you to do a little planning and preparation, possibly at the same cost or even at a savings compared to your current term life insurance. This is a short-term solution, good for only five years at a time. It might make sense to people in their 20's, 30's & 40's who can afford term life insurance but not Long-Term Care Insurance or whole life insurance.

9

Self-Funding

You've covered a lot of ground so far in this guide. You've seen that the government is very intent on getting you to pay for your own care, and you've read about all sorts of governmental incentives to purchase Long-Term Care Insurance. You've seen the cost of care and risk of needing care.

You've read about ways to best determine whether an insurance company will be financially stable enough in the future to pay benefits, and whether they have a good history of taking care of clients.

Still, many people simply don't like or trust insurance companies or agents, or are shocked when they see the premium for Long-Term Care Insurance. At that point they may say "it can't possibly be worth that much money. I'd rather set aside some money every month in a just-in-case, rainy day fund."

You may feel this way. This guide is here to help you make an informed decision, and it's my intent to cover all the bases when it comes to funding Long-Term Care. After all, this book's purpose is not to convince every reader to call for an insurance quote or appointment, or to convince you that insurance is always the answer.

Having said that, I'll prove that *self-funding as described above will never, and can't possibly, work better than purchasing Long-Term Care Insurance,* if you end up needing care even for a short time. Time to crunch some numbers!

Let's compare setting aside money each month at a predetermined rate of return, versus purchasing insurance.

Here are some real-world numbers, using a recent quote for "Jane Smith," age 55. Her quoted premium is $2,600 per year. This buys her a 4 year benefit of $5,000/month, with 4% compounded annual inflation protection included in her benefits. Four years is 48 months, times $5,000 equals a policy which is initially worth $240,000. Let's say Jane decides to invest the $2,600 premium each year instead of purchasing insurance, because she can never be 100% absolutely positive that she'll need care.

Jane sets these funds aside and tracks them separately from all her other investments, since this money is dedicated to pay for future care. Because these funds may be needed for care at any time, the principal can't be at risk in the stock market or mutual funds. In comparing self-funding to insurance funding for a future claim, she needs to guess at an average after-tax rate of return in an investment where her principal is not at risk. She decides 3% is the best possible return on her money, given the parameters above.

Next, she has to make a guess as to what age she'll potentially need care. She decides to be conservative and goes with 80 years old, which is 25 years in her future. She sets aside $216.67 per month, and invests the accumulated $2,600 at the end of the year. What if she has a claim right now? $2,600 wouldn't pay even one month in assisted living. Her policy would have been worth $249,600. You can start to see the problem: the value of her cash funds are of very little help in paying for care in the first 15-20 years.

Let's look at the numbers 25 years in the future - at age 80:

Her policy has increased in value at 4% per year and is now worth $639,800.72. The monthly benefit is $13,329.18. She's paid $65,000 in premiums. If she needs care for 5 months, she'll collect back everything she's paid in (not counting the time-value of her money if she'd invested it elsewhere).

She has diligently placed $2,600 per year in her account, and earned 3% after taxes, on average. Her self-funding account is now worth…$123,696.08. This is a pretty good chunk of change-but it only equals 10 months of policy benefits, if she'd purchased insurance. Her self-funding account is worth less than 20% of the hypothetical insurance policy. Remember, she had to average 3% after tax, and those funds were held sacrosanct from any purpose other than paying for care. To equal the value of the insurance policy, she would have had to self-fund $17.548.37 per year, rather than $2,600, or invest an initial lump sum of $305,572.39.

For her self-fund to equal the value of the hypothetical insurance policy at age 80, she would have had to earn an average return of over 16% after tax on her $2,600 deposits.

The reason the insurance policy is worth so much more at age 80 is simply that it started out with a value of $240,000, whereas her self-funding account started at $0. The insurance policy had a big head start-but that's how insurance works. If you like more detailed information, refer to the following table.

In a nutshell, the problem with self-funding is that you are likely to spend your retirement *principal* on care, during your golden years. Retirees live in income, not principal. If you spend principal on Long-Term Care, by selling property, cashing out IRA's, etc., to pay for care, you back yourself into a financial corner. Not to mention the possibility of losing 30-50% of your assets to taxes. Remember that neither the initial $240,000 policy benefit nor the $390,000 in growth to age 80 is taxable.

LONG-TERM CARE: SELF-FUNDING VS. INSURANCE POLICY FUNDING

				Age at time of claim:
Insured's name:	Jane Smith			
Insured's current age:	55			80
Annual policy premium:	$2,600.00			
Agent name:	Jeff Tomlin			

The value of your policy is calculated by multiplying the duration in months, times the monthly benefit. This value is commonly called the 'pool of money'.

	Duration	Monthly benefit
Policy duration & monthly benefit ---->	48	$5,000.00
Average monthly nursing home cost in Jane's state ---->	$8,610.00	At future age ----> $22,952.85
Average monthly assisted living cost in Jane's state ---->	$3,601.00	At future age ----> $9,599.68

"Long-Term Care Insurance Policy Account, Numbers and Information"

Your initial pool of money ----> $240,000.00	
Compound inflation protection amount ---->	4%
Pool of money size ---->	$639,800.72
Monthly benefit ---->	$13,329.18
Total premiums you've paid ---->	$65,000.00

"Self-Funding Account, Numbers and Information"

Average annual rate of return on your personally invested funds ---->	3%
The value of your self-funding account ---->	$123,696.08
Annual contribution to your self-funding account in order to equal 'pool of money', above: ---->	$17,548.37
	-OR-
Lump-sum initial contribution to your self-funding account in order to equal 'pool of money', above: ---->	$305,572.39

Average monthly nursing home cost in Jane's state at above future age is based on 4% compound inflation

10

Planning Workbook: Now the Rubber Meets the Road

How much care you should plan for, financially? How much money do you need to have set aside for care—now and in the future?

The first step is to determine how many years of care you should be prepared to pay for. My rule of thumb is to plan for a minimum of two years per spouse, but three years each is far better. Singles should plan on three to four years. Some Long-Term Care events last longer than average, of course: 20% last over 5 years. Also, remember that most of the time, people receive some care at home from loved ones before turning in a claim for Long-Term Care Insurance benefits. Statistically when it comes to Long-Term Care Insurance claims, 13.1 percent last more than three years, 7.6 percent last more than four years, and 4.5 percent last more than five years. From these statistics you can see that four years of protection will be enough for a single person the majority of the time, and six years of shared coverage for a couple will generally suffice to pay for average care needs for a couple. If there is a history of dementia, Alzheimer's, ALS, MS etc., in your family you may want to plan on a longer duration of care.

Next, you'll figure out how much money you should set aside for care. You'll follow two approaches to planning for Long-Term Care financing. The first is longer and likely more accurate; the second is "quick & dirty." One of the approaches will hopefully feel right to you.

You'll start the first calculation by taking another look at the "How Much Care Will You Need" table from longtermcare.gov. I mentioned earlier that the only problem with this table is that it has blended male and female statistics. The average duration of care for men is 2.2 years, and for women is 3.7 years. Add them together and divide by 2 and you get a "unisex" average duration of care, 3 years—shown in the second row of the table. I've added a fourth and fifth column. The fourth and fifth column use simple math to convert the unisex duration into male and female durations.

AVERAGE MALE AND FEMALE DURATION OF CARE

Type of care	Average number of years people use this type of care	Percent of people who use this type of care (%)	Male care duration by category (73% of average)	Female care duration by category (123% of average)
Any Services	3 years	69	2.2 years	3.7 years
At Home				
Unpaid care only*	1 year	59	*If you're single you'll need to plan on all "paid" care at home.	
Paid care	Less than 1 year	42		
Any care at home	2 years	65	1.5 years	2.5 years
In Facilities				
Nursing facilities	1 year	35		
Assisted living	Less than 1 year	13		
Any care in facilities	1 year	37	.7 years	1.2 years

Next you need to look up the cost of home care and facility care in your state. When you look at the following sources, consider using the cost for a private room rather than semi-private. Also, make sure you look up the numbers for the state in which you intend to retire, since the cost of care varies greatly from state to state. The average cost for various type of care as of 2012 in each state can be found in appendix one at the end of this book. A more accurate, online reference source is the 2012 Genworth cost of care map.[3] This map contains more current information than appendix one. In addition, the cost of care varies widely within each state. If you're able to go online to Genworth's map, you may find information more specific to your area.

Next we'll return to a modified version of the table from Longtermcare. gov. Complete it with the cost of care in your area (or the area in which you'll retire). I recommend using the nursing home cost for your facility care numbers. It's more conservative than using assisted living costs; you'll end up setting aside more money to pay for Long-Term Care.

Type of care	Male care duration	Yearly Cost of care in your area		Female care duration	Yearly Cost of care in your area	
Any care at home Use Genworth Cost of Care Map, Appendix 1. Multiply "Home Health Aide Hourly Rate" by 2,288. This is the cost for one year.	1.5 years	$ _____	Times 1.5 $ _____	2.5 years	$ _____	Times 2.5 $ _____
Any care in facilities (nursing home) Use Cost of Care Map, Appendix 1. Multiply "Nursing Home Private Room Rate" by 365. This is the cost for one year.	.7 years	$ _____	Times .7 $ _____	1.2 years	$ _____	Times 1.2 $ _____
Total, home plus facility care			$ _____			$ _____

Now you have a solid starting point. You can research Long-Term Care Insurance or hybrid policies if you wish, or set aside cash. If you take a look at hybrid life insurance, bear two things in mind: First, this makes more sense if your primary need is for life insurance, or you're on a budget which makes it difficult to purchase separate life and Long-Term Care Insurance policies. Secondly remember the primary upside and downside: You can buy a cash value policy in which your premium is guaranteed to never increase, but the policy's value will not go up over time to keep up with inflation.

Let's say private room nursing home care in your state is $100,000 per year, and home care is $40,000. If you're a woman, here's your formula based on the preceding table:

$100,000 x 1.2 + $40,000 x 2.5= $220,000.

For a man:

$100,000 x .7 + $40,000 x 1.5 = $130,000.

For a married couple who will purchase a policy with shared-care, add the male and female numbers up and divide by two:

$220,000 + $130,000 = $350,000.
Divided by 2, that equals $175,000 each.

You've now arrived at an initial requirement for finances, expressed as a dollar amount. Be aware that with few exceptions, when you shop for Long-Term Care Insurance you won't receive quotes for a specific dollar amount of coverage. Normally, insurance benefits are expressed as a monthly benefit and a given duration. For example the couple above who each need

$175,000 could ask for this quote: $5,000 per month for 3 years. $5,000 X 36 months = $180,000 each. Or $7,500 per month for 2 years each: $7,500 X 24 months = $180,000. The nationwide inflation rate for Long-Term Care has been about 4% over the last 5 years.[19] Purchasing 4 or 5% compound inflation protection for your policy, therefore, makes sense. A few companies also offer inflation protection which is based on the Consumer Price Index (CPI).

While any compound inflation protection will get you Partnership benefits if you reside in a Partnership state, here is the rest of the story. The older you are when you initially purchase a policy, the lower the requirement for purchasing inflation protection is on Long-Term Care Insurance. For most Partnership states, these are the requirements:

AGE AT TIME OF PURCHASE	MINIMUM REQUIRED LEVEL OF INFLATION PROTECTION
60 or younger	Any type of automatic inflation protection with annual compounding
61-75	Any type of automatic inflation protection with either annual compounding or simple
76 or older	No requirement

In the industry, we talk about "short-fat" and "long-thin" Long-Term Care Insurance plans. The first example on the prior page is longer and thinner and the second is shorter and fatter. 3 year benefit versus 2 year benefit. Consider a short-fat quote, especially if you're younger. One reason is because of the effect of compound inflation. Let's say the cost of care in your area right now is $8,000 per month. Thirty years from now assuming 4% inflation, the cost for that care will triple, to $24,000 per month. If you initially purchase a $5,000 per month benefit with 4% inflation protection, you might be able to pay the difference between the $8,000 actual cost and your $5,000 benefit with your own cash or pension. Unfortunately, 30 years later the cost is $24,000 and your benefit is $15,000. Now you have $9,000 per month out of pocket. Contrast this with the short-fat policy: your monthly benefit 30 years later has grown to $22,500, making it much easier to pay for the gap between policy benefits and the cost of care. Remember that if you are able to find care which costs less than your monthly benefit amount, your benefits will continue for a longer period of time.

The second method of planning for the financial cost of Long-Term Care reminds me of an old joke about taxes: your tax return form comes in the mail and you find it's been simplified. There is only one question on the first page: "how much did you earn"? You fill in the blank, and turn the page. The next page says "send it in."

This second method was suggested to me by a student in the Long-Term Care planning class I teach for the local community college. She had purchased a policy several years before. The advice she received at the time was "buy a policy equal in value to your net worth. Add inflation protection to the policy to cover the increase in your net worth over time."

The easiest way to determine your net worth is to simply subtract your debt from your assets. Use this next table for your calculation.

Add up the total net value of your assets, not including vehicles or household goods.	Retirement plans: IRA-401(k)-403(b)-457-TSA, etc.	Assets		Debts
	Bank accounts, CD's annuities, other cash, stock, bonds, investments.	$ _____	Student loans.	$ _____
	Life insurance cash value.	$ _____	Credit card balances.	$ _____
	Home equity.	$ _____	Car loans.	$ _____
	Enter these in the next column to the right, and total them at the bottom.	$ _____	Other debts.	$ _____
	Total assets	$ _____	**Total debt**	$ _____
Subtract total debts from total assets to determine your net worth				**Net worth** $ _____

This second method will probably work more often for you younger planners in your 40's and 50's or for any person or couple with a net worth of $200,000 to $500,000 or so. If your net worth is much higher and/or you're older, it might be difficult to purchase the larger amounts of insurance you'd need to cover 100% of your assets.

If you're still convinced that you want to self-fund Long-Term Care, use the numbers from the first method. In that example for a married couple, you'd need to have $350,000 cash on hand and earn 4-5% after tax return over time, to pay for care. But that $350,000 needs to be completely dedicated to pay for care and nothing else. Otherwise it shouldn't be counted as a Long-Term Care funding account. I'll say it **again**; if you have that much liquid money you could dedicate to care, why not buy insurance?

BRAINSTORMING

You've just reviewed two methods of figuring the cost of care. Perhaps neither of those methods feel like the right fit for you, perhaps they seem too much of a "one size fit's all" plan. Or maybe you already have insurance, but it's not enough. Your situation is unique and there's no reason to think that the "average" solution is the best one for you.

If you want to think outside of the box, read this next section. Hopefully it will get your creative juices flowing.

Here is a list of every possible funding solution I've mentioned, not counting those (governmental programs) that require your impoverishment prior to paying for care.

1. Reverse Mortgage

2. Long-Term Care Insurance

3. LTC Life Insurance (hybrid life)

4. LTC Annuities (hybrid annuity)

5. Impaired Risk Immediate Annuity (IIA)

6. Deferred Annuity (DA)

7. LTC-Friendly Universal Life Insurance (UL)

8. LTC-Friendly Term Life Insurance (TL)

9. Self-Funding (SF)

10. Life Settlements

11. Viatical Settlements

With all these tools, there should be something for everyone. Your stage in life, including your age, health, your assets, income, and your attitude about insurance and how to address risk, will make all the difference when it comes to choosing a funding solution.

Which funding solution will fit you best? Each person has different needs, assets, health, etc. On the next page you'll find a "health & wealth graph" which may give you some direction.

As with any other overhead or expense, you'll have to balance priorities.

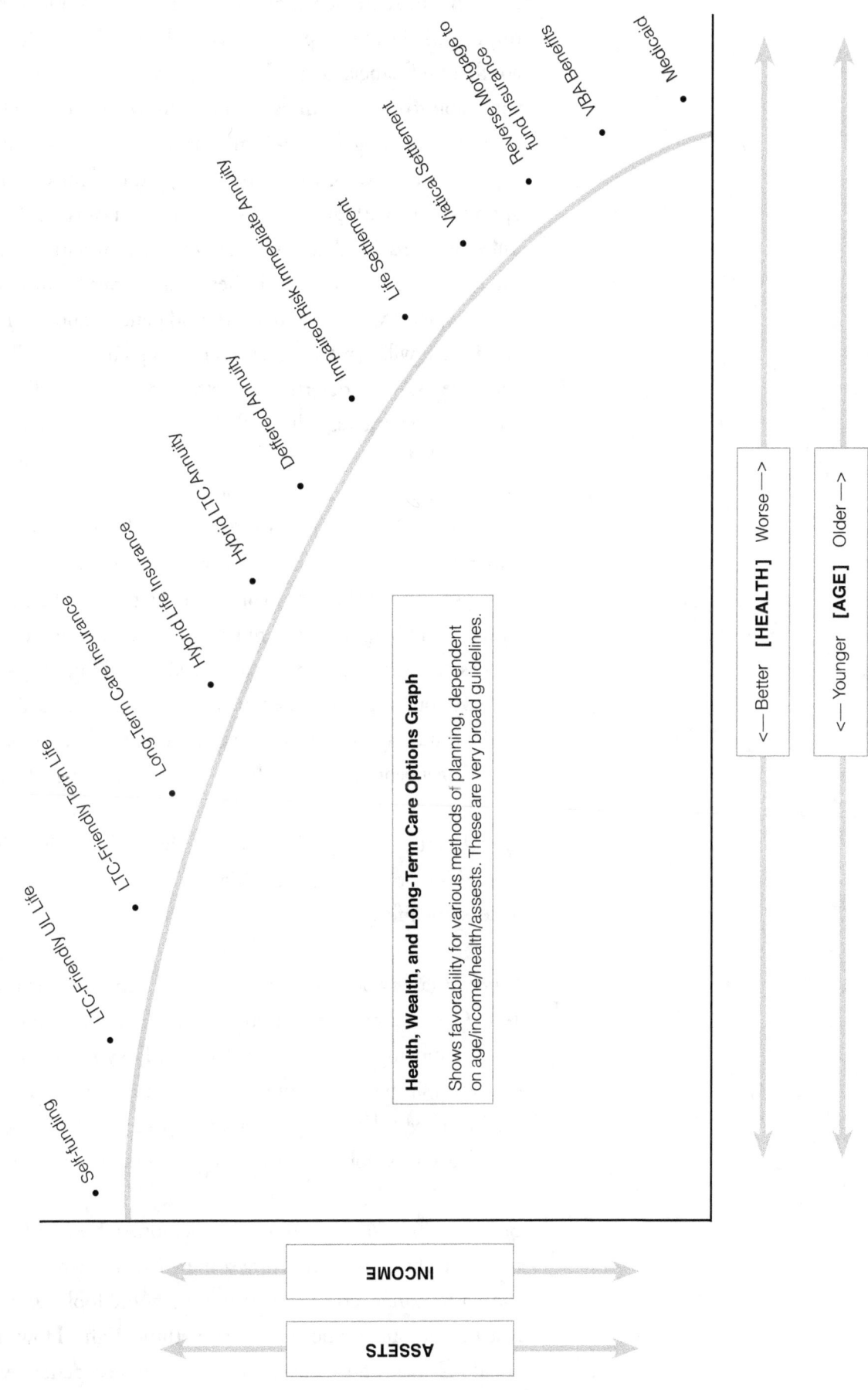

Health, Wealth, and Long-Term Care Options Graph

Shows favorability for various methods of planning, dependent on age/income/health/assests. These are very broad guidelines.

Self-funding

LTC-Friendly UL Life

LTC-Friendly Term Life

Long-Term Care Insurance

Hybrid Life Insurance

Hybrid LTC Annuity

Deferred Annuity

Impaired Risk Immediate Annuity

Life Settlement

Viatical Settlement

Reverse Mortgage to fund Insurance

VBA Benefits

Medicaid

<-- Better **[HEALTH]** Worse -->

<-- Younger **[AGE]** Older -->

INCOME

ASSETS

In saving for retirement, things like the cable TV bill, car payment, kid's tuition, and insurance premiums can slow us down. How can we balance conflicting financial goals? For the purposes of this book we will assume you're able to dedicate funds to address the risk of needing Long-Term Care.

Start by getting a Long-Term Care Insurance quote. Planning for care begins with knowing what a policy would cost for you. Prepare for your appointment with an agent—be aware you can't get an accurate quote unless you provide details such as your marital status, ten-year health history, your age, and so on. All these things affect your rates, and this generally explains why it's difficult to find generic quotes on the Internet. A good agent will scour several underwriting guides or call underwriters for you if necessary to determine whether you may qualify for coverage. The rates are the same regardless of which agent you get quotes from (they're approved/set by your state insurance commissioner), unless you qualify for an employer or association discount.

Now you have your quote. How does the premium look to you? Is it affordable? Would it fit the budget better if you took the inflation rider off? Perhaps this would be okay in order for you to get by for a few years. Perhaps this, in combination with some life insurance as mentioned above, would make sense. Just remember that generally speaking Long-Term Care Insurance without inflation protection is not Partnership qualified. Inflation protection on Long-Term Care Insurance is very, very, important—especially for younger people. On the other hand, something is far better than nothing!

Age 50. Perhaps a large whole life or universal life policy with a Long-Term Care rider would be suitable for you if separate Long-Term Care Insurance is not affordable.

Between 55 and 60. Your finances may be more stable now, so the Long-Term Care Insurance premium may fit your budget more easily. No? How about removing the inflation rider? No? Do you have a chunk of "just in case" cash sitting around, or CDs, or nonqualified annuities that you could roll into a hybrid life or hybrid annuity plan? No? How about a Long-Term Care Insurance policy with a smaller benefit or shorter duration?

Between 60 and 65. Are your finances more stable now? You're more likely to have a chunk of cash sitting somewhere, perhaps from an inheritance. Does the Long-Term Care Insurance quote look OK? Is it affordable? Maybe not, but you need to do something, right? How is your health? If you don't qualify for Long-Term Care Insurance, perhaps you'll still qualify for a hybrid life or hybrid annuity plan. Are you settled in your home? Is your mortgage paid off, or do you have a small balance left? How about refinancing into a reverse mortgage to improve cash flow? Does that provide the money you need to buy Long-Term Care Insurance or fund a hybrid policy? Cash value life insurance is a little expensive now, but perhaps it would make sense if you really want the death benefit of regular life insurance. Maybe you have CDs or annuities here or there, scattered around various accounts, or some inheritance money. You could combine those into a single large premium to pour into a hybrid product.

Between 65 and 75. Hopefully you're in good enough health to really enjoy yourself and stay active. If things have gone well, you have accumulated some cash to use in a hybrid plan. The average purchase age for Long-Term Care Insurance used to be in the late sixties. More recently, the age has dropped down to the mid fifties as awareness has risen. How does the Long-Term Care Insurance quote look? Is it affordable? Is the mortgage paid off? Are you settled in your house? How about getting quotes on a reverse mortgage and using those funds to leverage your dollars through a hybrid plan?

Between 75 and 80. How does the Long-Term Care Insurance quote look? Pretty high, I know. Definitely consider a plan without inflation protection at this point if the inflation protection is too expensive. Once you're over 75, you generally get Partnership benefits without inflation protection, so that's a plus. Is your mortgage paid off? This is a great time to check out the hybrid products, or perhaps a deferred annuity. Would your kids help you buy some Long-Term Care Insurance? They will if they're smart.

Beyond 80. Hybrid products and reverse mortgages may make more sense now. How is your health? Long-Term Care Insurance can be purchased through age 84, but it's very expensive and you have to be in fairly good health. How does the quote look to you? Is your mortgage paid off? Would you want to use your home equity as a source of funds for a hybrid product or Long-Term Care Insurance? Would your kids help you buy Long-Term Care Insurance? If you're in poor health but have a chunk of money available, how about looking at a deferred annuity? If you're in very poor health but have a chunk of money available and want income that is guaranteed to last the rest of your life, would it make sense to check out an impaired risk immediate annuity? Do you have any whole life insurance? A viatical or life settlement might look favorable to you, especially if you're uninsurable.

I hope that helps. Consider putting two or three different tools together and review your plan at least every five years to see if it needs revising.

Congratulations! You are forewarned and forearmed, and you have created a plan.

Now *take action*!

CONCLUSION

Everyone has a Long-Term Care plan. Sadly, those who have not made other arrangements are on the "default" plan. The default plan is to cash in retirement accounts, sell real property, etc., in order to pay for care after the need for care arises. At worst, this will continue until you become impoverished. At that point, Medicaid will probably help. For many, the default plan is the only option. It is certainly not a good plan for those who are in a position to have a say in the matter.

You've read that it is likely that you will need care. I hope that after reading this book, you now realize that you may have access to sources of funds you hadn't thought of prior to reviewing this material. Perhaps you have an old life insurance policy which can be sold, or you've discovered that you qualify for VA "aid and attendance" benefits. Maybe you've never considered a reverse mortgage before reading this book, but now you believe one may fit your needs. Unfortunately, these are low-percentage options. For most of us these options are not available, or they're not suitable given our circumstances.

Long-Term Care Insurance fits the broadest demographic of those who choose to plan ahead. If you do need care in the future, Long-Term Care Insurance is the least expensive way to pay for it. Remember, the early bird gets the worm! If you decide to shop for Long-Term Care Insurance, you need to do it while you're relatively young and healthy. When the time comes, your own cash & assets, your family, Medicaid, or insurance will pay for care. Which will it be?

This book presents a balanced overview, while attempting to persuade the reader of the need to plan ahead for Long-Term Care. My goal has been for you to reach your own conclusion on how to approach the issue, given the best information possible.

After reading this book, you may decide that Long-Term Care Insurance or some of the other insurance products reviewed herein have a place in your future. If so, keep me in mind.

Jeff Tomlin, CLTC
Tomlin Benefit Planning, Inc.   info@tbplan.com
Eugene OR 97401   www.tbplan.com/guidebook

About the Author

Jeff Tomlin lives in Oregon with 1 beautiful wife of 20 years, 2 daughters, 2 dogs, 2 cats, 18 chickens and 100,000 bees.

He graduated from Northwest Nazarene College in 1988 with a degree in mathematics. Holly and Jeff were married in 1992 and have two adopted daughters from the Philippines.

Jeff is passionate about planning ahead for Long-Term Care because of his own family history. It's his desire to help you avoid pitfalls. This book is the culmination of everything he's learned about Long-Term Care planning since 1994. It also rises out of the research he did while preparing to teach a Long-Term Care planning course at his local community college.

Because of personal exposure to the pain of a Long-Term Care event, and after learning the statistics, he is convinced that everyone who is able should plan ahead for eventual care.

Jeff started his insurance career in 1988 and sold his first Long-Term Care Insurance policy, to his father, in 1994. He is Partnership trained, and is a member of the American Association for Long Term Care Insurance (AALTCI). He achieved his CLTC (Certified in Long Term Care) credentialing in 2009.

Guide to Abbreviations

ACA	Affordable Care Act of 2010	ICF	intermediate care facility	TQ	tax qualified
ADL	activities of daily living	IIA	impaired-risk immediate annuity	UL	universal life insurance
AFH	adult foster home	LTCi	Long-Term Care Insurance	VA	Veterans Administration
ALF	assisted living facility			VBA	Veterans Benefits Administration
CI	chronic illness	PPA	Pension Protection Act of 2006	VHA	Veterans Health Administration
CLASS	Community Living Assistance Services and Supports Act	RCF	residential care facility		
DA	deferred annuity	RN	registered nurse		
DRA	Deficit Reduction Act	SF	self-funding		
HIPPA	Health Insurance Privacy and Portability Accountability Act of 1996	SNF	skilled nursing facility		
		TI	terminal illness		
		TL	term life insurance		

Appendix 1

State-by-state cost of care, from Genworth's 2012 cost of care survey

State	Homemaker Services Hourly Rate (Licensed)*	Home Health Aide Hourly Rate (Licensed)	Adult Day Health Care (Daily Rates)	Assisted Living Facility (Monthly Rates)	Nursing Home Daily Rate (Semi-Private Room)	Nursing Home Daily Rate (Private Room)†
Alabama	$16	$16	$25	$2,948	$175	$180
Alaska	$24	$25	$104	$5,500	$750	$637
Arizona	$19	$20	$82	$3,100	$186	$226
Arkansas	$17	$17	$64	$2,810	$147	$161
California	$21	$23	$77	$3,500	$224	$258
Colorado	$20	$21	$62	$3,703	$206	$231
Connecticut	$19	$21	$75	$4,475	$370	$400
Delaware	$21	$23	$75	$5,269	$250	$265
Florida	$17	$18	$59	$2,750	$215	$232
Georgia	$17	$17	$60	$2,500	$163	$175
Hawaii	$22	$25	$67	$3,750	$320	$345
Idaho	$18	$19	$96	$3, 214	$200	$220
Illinois	$20	$20	$65	$4,057	$164	$190
Indiana	$18	$19	$65	$3,620	$187	$225
Iowa	$20	$21	$53	$2,939	$152	$167
Kansas	$18	$18	$70	$3,501	$150	$165
Kentucky	$17	$17	$59	$2,741	$189	$207

State	Homemaker Services Hourly Rate (Licensed)*	Home Health Aide Hourly Rate (Licensed)	Adult Day Health Care (Daily Rates)	Assisted Living Facility (Monthly Rates)	Nursing Home Daily Rate (Semi-Private Room)	Nursing Home Daily Rate (Private Room)†
Louisiana	$15	$15	$60	$3,100	$141	$155
Maine	$20	$22	$96	$4,500	$264	$288
Maryland	$19	$20	$76	$3,200	$244	$263
Massachusetts	$23	$25	$61	$4,588	$322	$350
Michigan	$19	$20	$71	$2,713	$220	$240
Minnesota	$22	$25	$75	$3,136	$210	$234
Mississippi	$17	$17	$50	$2,925	$196	$205
Missouri	$18	$18	$72	$2, 419	$139	$152
Montana	$19	$21	$80	$3,150	$193	$206
Nebraska	$19	$21	$53	$3,250	$176	$193
Nevada	$20	$21	$66	$2,995	$220	$240
New Hampshire	$23	$24	$63	$4,000	$270	$288
New Jersey	$20	$21	$80	$5,713	$292	$315
New Mexico	$18	$20	$112	$3,500	$185	$207
New York	$20	$22	$55	$3,700	$325	$337
North Carolina	$17	$18	$52	$2,900	$190	$210
North Dakota	$24	$24	$53	$2,730	$206	$221
Ohio	$19	$19	$50	$3,713	$200	$223
Oklahoma	$17	$19	$53	$2,751	$135	$147
Oregon	$20	$21	$97	$3,850	$225	$250
Pennsylvania	$20	$20	$55	$3, 251	$251	$272
Rhode Island	$20	$24	$71	$3,898	$250	$315
South Carolina	$17	$18	$50	$2,875	$180	$195
South Dakota	$20	$20	$29	$2,746	$180	$188
Tennessee	$17	$17	$55	$3,304	$180	$191
Texas	$17	$18	$34	$3,200	$130	$169
Utah	$20	$21	$45	$2,650	$160	$185
Vermont	$21	$21	$132	$3,900	$252	$278
Virginia	$18	$18	$55	$3,481	$198	$225
Washington	$22	$22	$59	$4,250	$240	$265
West Virginia	$15	$16	$52	$3,000	$230	$242
Wisconsin	$20	$21	$58	$3,700	$229	$255
Wyoming	$20	$21	$56	$3,298	$198	$220

* Multiply by 44 (hours of care per week), and by 52 (weeks in a year) to figure the annual cost for this type of care.
† Multiply by 365 (days in a year) to figure the annual cost of care.

Appendix 2

The "itsmylifekit"

This planning guide focuses on the financial cost of Long-Term Care. For direction with other, "later-in-life" planning, such as advanced directives, power of attorney, wills and trusts, and much, much more, I recommend the It's My Life Kit. This wonderful resource is a reminder of the planning which needs to happen, as well as a repository for the various documents & information you'll accumulate. It will also help you organize all the information your family members need in case you're unable to speak to them at some time in the future. Here are just a few of the items it will help you consider:

- Do you have a safety deposit box? Where do you keep the key?

- Who will help you with transportation when you can't drive?

- Who will care for your pets and tend to your lawn, mail, newspaper, garbage, and household chores if you're unable?

Visit **www.itsmylifekit.com** or email **info@itsmylifekit.com** for more information about this helpful repository.

Appendix 3

Inflation table

End of year	Inflation of $10,000 at 3% <u>simple</u>	Inflation of $10,000 at 3% compound	Inflation of $10,000 at 3.5% compound	Inflation of $10,000 at 4% compound	Inflation of $10,000 at 4.5% compound	Inflation of $10,000 at 5% compound	Inflation of $10,000 at 5% <u>simple</u>
1	$10,300	$10,300	$10,350	$10,400	$10,450	$10,500	$10,500
2	$10,600	$10,609	$10,712	$10,816	$10,920	$11,025	$11,000
3	$10,900	$10,927	$11,087	$11,249	$11,412	$11,576	$11,500
4	$11,200	$11,255	$11,475	$11,699	$11,925	$12,155	$12,000
5	$11,500	$11,593	$11,877	$12,167	$12,462	$12,763	$12,500
6	$11,800	$11,941	$12,293	$12,653	$13,023	$13,401	$13,000
7	$12,100	$12,299	$12,723	$13,159	$13,609	$14,071	$13,500
8	$12,400	$12,668	$13,168	$13,686	$14,221	$14,775	$14,000
9	$12,700	$13,048	$13,629	$14,233	$14,861	$15,513	$14,500
10	$13,000	$13,439	$14,106	$14,802	$15,530	$16,289	$15,000
11	$13,300	$13,842	$14,600	$15,395	$16,229	$17,103	$15,500
12	$13,600	$14,258	$15,111	$16,010	$16,959	$17,959	$16,000
13	$13,900	$14,685	$15,640	$16,651	$17,722	$18,856	$16,500
14	$14,200	$15,126	$16,187	$17,317	$18,519	$19,799	$17,000
15	$14,500	$15,580	$16,753	$18,009	$19,353	$20,789	$17,500
16	$14,800	$16,047	$17,340	$18,730	$20,224	$21,829	$18,000
17	$15,100	$16,528	$17,947	$19,479	$21,134	$22,920	$18,500
18	$15,400	$17,024	$18,575	$20,258	$22,085	$24,066	$19,000
19	$15,700	$17,535	$19,225	$21,068	$23,079	$25,270	$19,500

End of year	Inflation of $10,000 at 3% simple	Inflation of $10,000 at 3% compound	Inflation of $10,000 at 3.5% compound	Inflation of $10,000 at 4% compound	Inflation of $10,000 at 4.5% compound	Inflation of $10,000 at 5% compound	Inflation of $10,000 at 5% simple
20	$16,000	$18,061	$19,898	$21,911	$24,117	$26,533	$20,000
21	$16,300	$18,603	$20,594	$22,788	$25,202	$27,860	$20,500
22	$16,600	$19,161	$21,315	$23,699	$26,337	$29,253	$21,000
23	$16,900	$19,736	$22,061	$24,647	$27,522	$30,715	$21,500
24	$17,200	$20,328	$22,833	$25,633	$28,760	$32,251	$22,000
25	$17,500	$20,938	$23,632	$26,658	$30,054	$33,864	$22,500
26	$17,800	$21,566	$24,460	$27,725	$31,407	$35,557	$23,000
27	$18,100	$22,213	$25,316	$28,834	$32,820	$37,335	$23,500
28	$18,400	$22,879	$26,202	$29,987	$34,297	$39,201	$24,000
29	$18,700	$23,566	$27,119	$31,187	$35,840	$41,161	$24,500
30	$19,000	$24,273	$28,068	$32,434	$37,453	$43,219	$25,000
31	$19,300	$25,001	$29,050	$33,731	$39,139	$45,380	$25,500
32	$19,600	$25,751	$30,067	$35,081	$40,900	$47,649	$26,000
33	$19,900	$26,523	$31,119	$36,484	$42,740	$50,032	$26,500
34	$20,200	$27,319	$32,209	$37,943	$44,664	$52,533	$27,000
35	$20,500	$28,139	$33,336	$39,461	$46,673	$55,160	$27,500

End Notes

1. See http://www.caregiver.org/

2. From Genworth's "Beyond Dollars" (See #4).

3. http://seniorliving.about.com/od/healthnutrition/a/caregivertips.htm

4. Beyond Dollars (link is at the bottom right of the page): https://www.genworth.com/dam/Americas/US/PDFs/Consumer/corporate/Beyond%20Dollars%20FINAL%20109048_093010_secure.pdf

5. http://www.longtermcare.gov/LTC/Main_Site/Planning/Importance/How_Much.aspx

6. http://www.longtermcare.gov/LTC/Main_Site/Planning/Importance/How_Much.aspx. See also http://www.aarp.org/relationships/caregiving/info-2007/fs27r_ltc.html

7. See http://www.genworth.com/content/genworth/us/en/products/long_term_care/long_term_care/cost_of_care.html

8. http://www.cbsnews.com/8301-505146_162-39941582/tips-for-buying-long-term-care-insurance/?tag=mwuser

9. http://medicaidbenefits.kff.org/

10. http://www.longtermcare.gov/LTC/Main_Site/Paying/Costs/Who_Pays.aspx

11. http://www.vba.va.gov/bln/21/pension/ State VA office directory: http://www.va.gov/statedva.htm

12. The numbers in these examples are based on reverse-mortgage quotes from April 2011.

13. http://www.reversemortgage.org/

14. For more information, visit http://w2.dehpg.net/LTCPartnership/map.aspx. To view a PDF document with information on each state's Partnership program, visit http://w2.dehpg.net/LTCPartnership/images/State%20Matrices.pdf.

15. For a list of tax-deductibility rules, state by state, go here: http://www.aaltci.org/long-term-care-insurance/learning-center/tax-for-business.php#state

16. Available at http://insurance.oregon.gov/publications/consumer/2311-11.pdf

17. To see your states' limits: http://www.aaltci.org/long-term-care-insurance/learning-center/state-insurance-guaranty.php

18. http://www.aaltci.org/subpages/resources/claimsreport.pdf

19. http://www.genworth.com/content/etc/medialib/genworth_v2/pdf/ltc_cost_of_care.Par.40001.File.dat/2012%20Cost%20of%20Care%20Survey%20Full%20Report.pdf